WOODWORKING
AND FURNITURE MAKING
FOR THE HOME

Woodworking and Furniture Making

for the Home

G. W. ENDACOTT DLC

Illustrations by the author

David & Charles : Newton Abbot : Devon

ISBN 0 7153 5387 X

To my parents

*Set in 11/12-point Baskerville
and printed in Great Britain
by W J Holman Limited Dawlish Devon
for David & Charles (Publishers) Limited
South Devon House Newton Abbot Devon*

Contents

Illustrations

Chapter 1

Basic Essentials

THE WORKSHOP

There are many difficulties in using the same building as both workshop and garage, or workshop and garden shed. A separate workshop is preferable, though often one has little choice. It is a consoling fact that many fine pieces of work have been constructed under conditions far short of ideal.

The workshop should be large enough to store tools and materials easily in an uncluttered way. It should be possible to use the bench without constantly having to rearrange things. The ceiling should be high enough so that an assembled article can be placed on the bench without hindrance, and there should be sufficient floor space to contain racks for all hand tools. Tools are best stored under the bench or upon the wall so that the floor space is kept to a maximum. Orderly tool racks provide safety and accessibility.

Careful planning is required to make sure the workshop can contain all the items required. If more than one person is to use the room at a time then machinery must be placed well away from the benches. It is important to leave a clear space for the unhindered passage of timber through a machine. The workshop must have places allocated to store tools and timber, to glue-up, to sharpen tools; or alternative arrangements must be made for these activities. If the bench is to serve for sharpening and glueing-up this must be planned into the scheme from an early stage.

The roof and walls of the building should be insulated if they are of light construction, so that the room is reasonably warm in winter yet remains cool in summer. A safe form of heating must be considered for the winter months. The building must be dry inside in order that tools do not rust and timber does not change its shape unduly. A large door is important. Remember that large sheets of plywood and planks of timber will on occasion need to be brought in. For this reason double opening doors are advantageous.

Large windows will provide good, natural lighting on the workspace. Artificial lighting required during the evening and on dull winter days should be provided by an ordinary electric light bulb. Fluorescent lighting should be avoided as it makes the colours false and flattens the appearance of the work because it shows no shadows. It is a good idea to consider siting the workshop in such a position that electricity for lighting and power can be connected without difficulty. Hot and cold running water are also useful.

A wooden floor is better than concrete. Sharp edge tools dropped on such a floor are unlikely to chip or blunt, and steel planes are less likely to break. A wooden floor is also more pleasant to stand on and is warmer in winter. However, the floor must be firm and give good support to the bench so that heavy work such as chopping out large mortises can be carried out effectively on the bench top.

THE BENCH

The woodwork bench is an essential part of the equipment. Figure 1 shows the typical arrangement of a traditional bench.

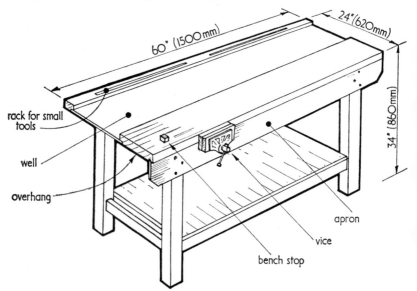

Fig 1 The woodwork bench

The Lervad bench, of Scandinavian design, is shown in plate 1. Either type of bench would be suitable for the work described in this book.

The sketch shows the principal dimensions for a bench. The most important size shown is the height. If the bench is not at the correct height then it will be found uncomfortable to work at for a lengthy period. A tall person will require a bench that is a little higher than the one shown and a short person will require a bench that is lower. As a general rule it is best to have the height of the working surface the length of a chisel below the level of the elbow. This allows the person to work as comfortably on the top of the bench as at the vice.

The parts of the bench which are indicated in figure 1 have various functions that may not be apparent at first sight. The well is the place to put tools that are needed to hand in the immediate future. The proper place for tools when they are not being used is in a rack, but they may be laid down temporarily in the well, where there is little fear of them rolling off onto the floor.

The apron is a wide board running the length of the front. This is notched around the legs and secured in place by screws. It makes the construction rigid and prevents a see-saw motion of the bench when planing a piece of wood.

The bench stop prevents the work from sliding off during planing. It is a block of wood that projects above the bench top. Figure 2 shows how the bench stop is adjusted by use of a wing nut.

The bench must have an overhang at the end for cramping wood when sawing or chiselling. The top is $1\frac{3}{4}$in (45mm) thick and is usually made of a solid piece of beechwood to give good support to the work. This way the energy produced by blows of the mallet upon a chisel is not lost in the spring of the bench. Look after the top of the bench because if it is worn hollow by tool marks then it cannot be expected to support the work when planing flat. It must be remembered that the bench is a tool and should be treated with the respect given to other tools.

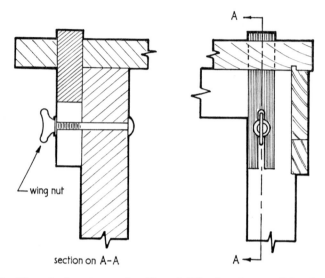

Fig 2 How the bench stop is adjusted. The bench stop slides through a hole in the bench top and is held in position by a wing nut and bolt

THE VICE

The vice is the most important part of the whole equipment needed in a workshop. A jaw width of 7in (180mm) and opening of 8in (200mm) will be found adequate for most work. To open the vice to maximum aperture one has to turn the handle many times. An improved vice, fitted with a quick release lever, saves time. With this lever pressed the vice can be opened by pulling the jaw straight out. However, this vice is more expensive and for the kind of work envisaged in this book the quick release mechanism is in no way essential.

The jaws of the vice should be lined with wooden packing to prevent bruising the work. Countersink bolts can be bought to fit the two threaded holes provided in each jaw and may be used to hold the wooden packing in place.

The portable vice is a handy temporary measure. It can be easily fitted to a table by tightening the screw underneath, and when work is finished for the day the vice can be removed with equal ease to be stored elsewhere. This tool could be useful to those people who have very limited space to establish a workshop, but for the sort of work envisaged in this book the plain screw woodworkers' vice will be found more serviceable.

THE BENCH TOOLS

The nine bench tools that are most commonly used are best located near to hand in a rack fitted to the bench or fastened to the wall directly above it.

☐ STEEL RULE

The steel rule should be about 12in (300mm) long. The rule has two uses in the workshop: first, and most obvious, measuring, and second, checking the work for flatness. To check for flatness place the edge of the rule on the work and arrange the light behind the work. Gaps that show between the rule and the surface of the work are hollows. It will be seen that the markings on the steel rule start from the very end. There is no extra piece as on most wooden rulers. This enables one to measure accurately into a corner, for instance when measuring the inside depth of a drawer. The end of a steel rule is not liable to wear so the rule remains true. Its edges will also remain straight and accurate for a very long time. Figure 3 shows how to check a rule for straightness.

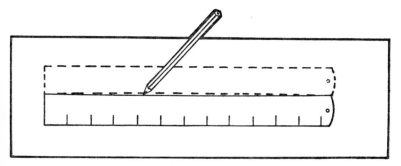

Fig 3 Testing the steel rule for straightness. Mark against the edge with a sharp pencil and then turn the rule over and repeat, a trick that 'doubles' any discrepancy

◻ TRY SQUARE

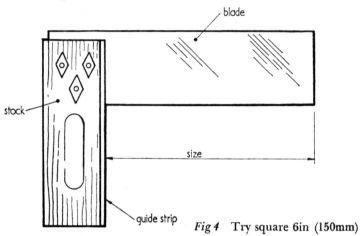

Fig 4 Try square 6in (150mm)

The try square consists of two main parts: the steel blade and the stock, which is made from rosewood. These two parts are fastened together by three steel rivets. The ends of each rivet are fitted with a diamond-shaped brass washer to prevent the rivet from splitting the stock. A brass guide strip on the inside edge of the stock prevents the rosewood from wearing. This tool must be handled with care and never dropped if it is to retain its accuracy.

The try square is used to check if one surface of the work is at right angles to another. It may also be used as a guide when

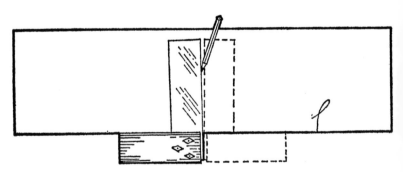

Fig 5 Checking a try square for squareness. Place the square against a straight edge and mark with a sharp pencil. Reverse the square and repeat. The marks will coincide only if the square is accurate

marking lines across the wood at right angles to an edge. Figure 5 shows how to check a try square for squareness. Any inaccuracy can be corrected by judicious use of the file. A handy size for the try square is 6in (150mm).

☐ MARKING KNIFE

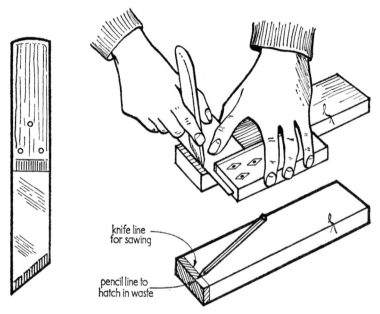

knife line
for sawing

pencil line to
hatch in waste

Fig 6 Marking knife and how it is used. Grip the knife like a pencil and hold it upright. Pull the knife towards the person to make a clean line

The marking knife has a steel blade and a handle made of either beechwood or rosewood. The two parts are held together by three rivets. The knife is used to mark all lines that are to be sawn, whereas the pencil is used for hatching waste, numbering joints, and marking shaping on the wood. The advantage of the marking knife over the pencil is that it produces a more accurate mark on the wood and also severs the fibres of the grain in advance of the saw. The knife is used in an upright position and pulled firmly against the try square. The knife is held by the blade rather than the handle. It should be

B

kept sharp so as to produce a clean cut. A small penknife will always serve as a marking knife. Remember to use a marking knife for lines that are to be sawn.

☐   TENON SAW

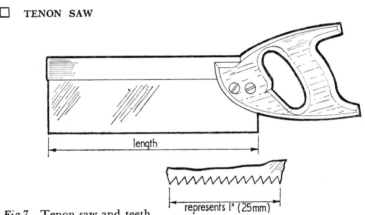

length

represents 1" (25mm)

Fig 7   Tenon saw and teeth

The tenon saw is used for sawing accurately to length and for general bench work. As its name implies it is used also for sawing the tenon of the mortise and tenon joint. This saw is about 10in (250mm) long. The handle is made from beechwood and the thin blade is cold rolled steel stiffened by a back of brass or steel. For this reason the tenon saw belongs to a family of saws called *backed saws*. The handle is fastened to the blade by two saw bolts.

The sketch shows that there are fourteen points per inch on the tenon saw. Obviously the more teeth there are the smaller they are. The teeth can be made so small they become difficult to sharpen. The number of points per inch mentioned here is considered adequate for general bench work.

The bench hook is used to support the wood when cutting across the grain with a tenon saw. It should be made from hard wood—beech or oak—for a long life. The two blocks are fastened to the base by wooden dowels instead of screws so that the teeth of the saw may not be damaged. It will be noticed that the block of the bench hook is short on the right-hand side. This is to provide protection for the bench top and prevent the saw making any marks on the bench. Because of this

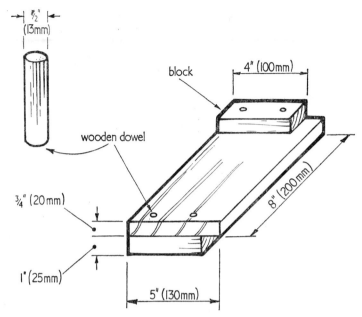

Fig 8 Construction of a bench hook. Made from beechwood and fastened with dowels, the bench hook should have a long and serviceable life

the bench hook shown in figure 8 is only suitable for a right-handed person. A left-handed person should remove part of the left-hand end of the block.

In use the bench hook can be made firm by clamping the lower block in the vice. The wood is then placed across the bench hook and gripped tightly against the front block by the palm and fingers of the left hand. Grip the tenon saw firmly, with the forefinger outside the handle and pointing forward. This will ensure positive control over the saw. Start the cut on the far corner of the wood. Guide the saw by the thumb of the left hand and draw the saw backwards three times to make a groove on the corner of the work. Then commence sawing and lower the handle of the saw with each stroke until the saw is horizontal. Normally one is following a line on the wood and as the saw is brought into the horizontal position the line is watched carefully to give an accurately positioned cut. At this stage one's head should be directly over the line. Looking down, both sides of the saw should be seen at once. If this is not the case then the saw is not being held upright. Move the saw until both sides of the blade can be seen. Check most care-

Fig 9 Starting a cut with the tenon saw. The thumb positions the blade as the saw is drawn backwards three times on the corner of the wood

fully that the saw is held upright. When all is correct continue sawing. Use all the teeth of the saw by making long steady strokes. This way the saw will stay sharp for a long time. Take the last three strokes more slowly until the cut is completed. The end of the work should be sawn sufficiently square that the piece can be stood upright on the cut surface.

☐ FIRMER CHISEL (fig 31)

The firmer chisel is used for general bench work. The handle is shaped into a comfortable grip for pushing the chisel into the work. The blade is fastened to the handle by the tang. The shoulder prevents the tang from pushing too far into the handle. The ferrule is a seamless ring of brass or steel and it prevents the tang from splitting the handle. A handy size of chisel for bench work has a blade that is $\frac{5}{8}$in (16mm) wide.

Three safety rules apply when using a chisel. Firstly, always keep the cutting edge sharp. Sharp tools are less dangerous than blunt ones. A blunt chisel has to be forced to make it cut and when forcing the tool into the work it is easy to be taken off balance if the wood splits, or when the chisel reaches the end of the cut. Secondly, always cut away from the body. Keep all fingers behind the cutting edge. Hold the handle of the chisel in the right hand and the blade between the thumb and forefinger of the left hand. This way there is good control over the chisel and there is no risk of cutting oneself should a slip occur. Thirdly, always carry a chisel by the blade and near the cutting edge. Should someone nearby not realise there is a chisel in your hand and step back quickly, they are thus protected from the cutting edge.

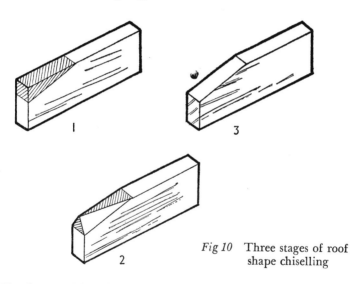

Fig 10   Three stages of roof
shape chiselling

The firmer chisel is used frequently for shaping wood held in the vice, and for vertical paring on the bench. All the marking out should be done first with pencil. Then place the piece of wood in the vice at such an angle that the line representing the finished surface is horizontal. Select a large chisel and hold it with the axis horizontal and the cutting edge tilted to 45°. Start by removing a small shaving from the top of the work as shown in figure 11. Note that one should stand half way along the side and work towards the left end of the bench. One only works in the opposite direction if left-handed.

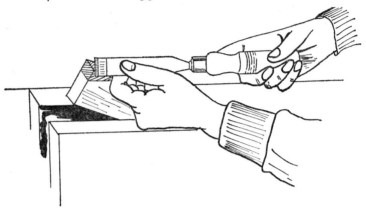

Fig 11   Starting the cut. The work is held firmly in the vice, allowing both hands to grasp the chisel, as shown

Continue to chisel working down to the finished line until only the line itself is left. Then tilt the cutting edge of the chisel to 45° the other way and tackle the second side of the work. It will be apparent why this is called *roof shape chiselling*. It only remains to remove the ridge of the roof with the chisel and the shape is completed.

Vertical paring is used when rounding the corners of the wood or making a small 45° cut across the corner as shown in figure 12. Use a coin or tin lid of suitable curve as a template when drawing the shape on the wood. Lines are squared across the edges of the work to mark the exact limit of the curve. The waste is hatched in with a pencil.

The work is laid flat on a chiselling board. This is simply a smooth piece of wood laid on the bench to protect the surface of the bench from chisel marks. The handle of the chisel is held in the right hand with the thumb on top. The thumb and forefinger of the left hand guide the blade of the chisel. The left hand is placed on the work to hold it in position.

Start work on the corner of the wood by pushing down on the chisel. Take a modest cut and there should be no reason to hit the chisel with a mallet. This cut will create two corners which can be removed in turn. The work continues and the

line is approached gradually. The many facets made by the
chisel will form the curve.

With the straight 45° cut work starts on the corner of the
wood and the chisel is moved back to the line in stages. The

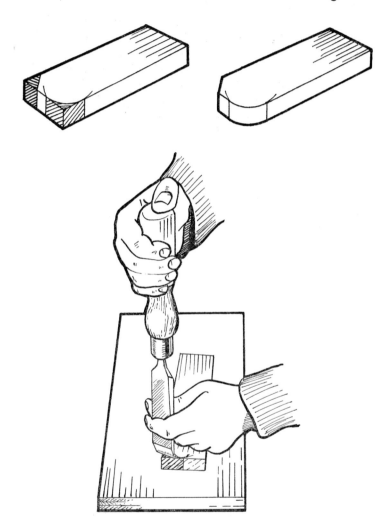

Fig 12 Vertical paring. All marking for shaping is done with a pencil.
Support the work on a chiselling board and hold the chisel as shown.
Keep fingers behind the cutting edge and take modest cuts

shavings taken are forever increasing in width. The last cut is made on the line.

☐   MARKING GAUGE

The marking gauge consists of four parts: stock. stem, thumbscrew and spur. The stock and stem are made of beech-wood, which is hardwearing. The thumbscrew is sometimes made of boxwood because this is such a fine grained wood that it can be threaded, but boxwood is being superseded by plastic. The steel spur is sharpened to a point. The marking gauge is used for marking a line that is parallel to an edge. It is always used with the grain of the wood.

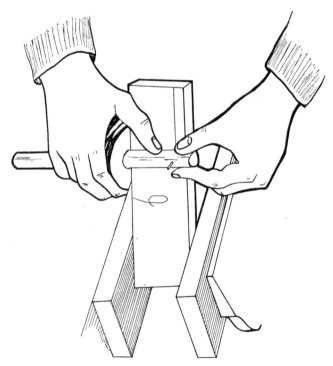

Fig 13   Using the marking gauge. Hold the wood in the vice and keep the gauge tightly against the face edge

☐ JACK PLANE

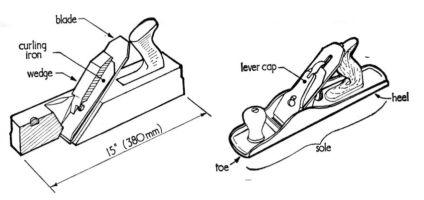

Fig 14 Wooden and metal jack planes. The wooden jack plane *(left)* is shown in part section

The jack plane is used chiefly to remove a lot of waste as quickly as possible. It receives its name from the expression *jack of all trades.* There are two types of jack plane. One is made of metal, the other of beechwood. Both planes are 15in (380mm) long. The wooden plane is lighter and therefore easier to use over a long period. It also slides over the surface of the work better than a metal plane and therefore requires less effort. Another advantage of the wooden plane is that it is less likely to break if dropped. Despite these three advantages, the metal plane is still the more popular because it is easy to adjust.

Figure 14 shows the chief parts of the plane. The blade cuts the shavings from the work and the curling iron curls the shavings, thereby preventing tears (pronounced 'tares') on the surface of the wood. The blade and curling iron are fastened together by a large screw, and the pair of irons are retained in the body of the planes by either a wooden wedge, as in the case of the wooden plane, or a lever cap in the case of the metal plane.

When using the plane the wood should be placed against the bench stop, although the vice may be used when planing the narrow edge of a piece of timber that will not stand properly on top of the bench. Take an easy but firm position

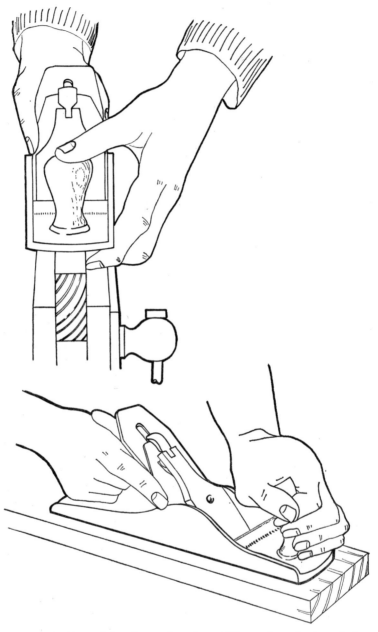

Fig 15 Position of hands on the plane. When edge planing timber, the fingers can act as a guide

directly behind the work. Stand at the side of the bench and work towards the end. Figure 15 shows the position of the hands on the plane. The chief function of the right hand is to push the plane forward. It is the left hand that presses down and holds the plane on the wood. When planing a narrow edge let the fingers of the left hand act as a fence under the sole of the plane, guiding the work to the centre position of the cutter. Start each cut by pressing down firmly at the toe of the plane with the left hand. Push the plane along the wood with the right hand but release the pressure applied to the front of the plane towards the end of the stroke. If the wood tears it is because the plane is being used against the grain. In this case turn the wood around and plane from the other end of the work.

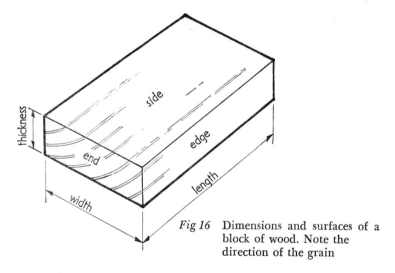

Fig 16   Dimensions and surfaces of a block of wood. Note the direction of the grain

The beginner will often round over the end of the work. To avoid this a pencil mark can be made about 1in (25mm) in from each end of the wood. Place the plane on the work so that the cutter avoids the first mark, and remove one shaving up to the second mark. Continue planing in this matter until the plane stops cutting. The work has now been planed slightly hollow but the plane will not make a deeper hollow because it rests on the high parts at each end. Finally, remove one shaving from the length of the work. This will remove most of the high parts at the ends.

The side of the wood that has just been planed is called the *face side* and should be marked in pencil with the symbol shown (fig 17). This symbol is called the *face side mark* and it points to the best edge called the *face edge*. The object of planing the face edge is to produce a flat smooth surface at right angles to the face side. Check for flatness with the steel rule then check for squareness with the try square. Place the stock of the square against the face side of the work and hold it up to the light. Again, any gaps that show are hollows. Look for the high parts and mark these with a pencil. The cutter of the jack plane is slightly rounded. Move the plane over so that the thickest part of the shaving will be taken from the highest part of the edge. When the face edge is correct mark it with a face edge mark pointing to the face side.

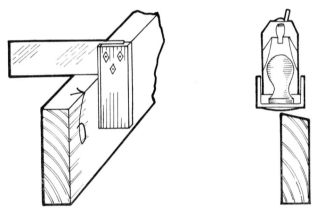

Fig 17 Checking for squareness and planing square. Check from the face side. Move the plane over to correct as the thickest shaving is cut from the centre of the cutter

The piece of wood has now been planed on two surfaces. In order that the work finishes parallel a line must be marked on the wood parallel to the face edge. Set the marking gauge to the width of wood required. Measure the size from the stock of the gauge to the point of the spur (fig 18). Hold the gauge by the stock and tap the stem on the bench to make fine adjustments if necessary.

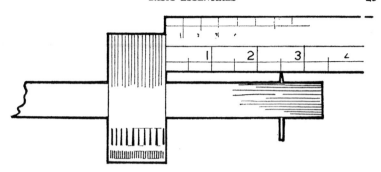

Fig 18 Setting a marking gauge. Measure from the stock to the
point of the spur

Place the wood in the vice face edge towards the centre of
the bench, and slope the wood to 45° before tightening the
vice jaw. Put the stock of the gauge against the face edge and
hold the gauge with both hands. Press the gauge tightly against
the face edge and tilt so that the spur trails behind as the tool
is pushed slowly along. People often forget that the object of
using a gauge is to produce a line that is parallel to an edge,
so hold the gauge tightly against the work.

Turn the wood end for end in the vice and mark the line all
the way around. Always take care to use the gauge from the
face edge so that the gauge line is nearest the rough edge of
the wood.

Look at the wood before planing down to the line. If there
is greater waste at one end than the other then shavings will
have to be planed off the high point first. Otherwise there is a
tendency to plane past the line at one end of the work (fig 19).
Check for flatness with a steel rule and squareness with a try
square.

Finally, gauge to thickness from the face side. Plane to
thickness and test for flatness.

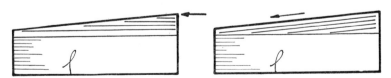

Fig 19 Planing to width correctly *(left)* and incorrectly *(right)*

Planing a piece of wood takes time and skill. It is therefore recommended that most wood be bought ready planed by machine. However, knowing how to plane a piece of wood square will be found advantageous. The method may be summarised by the four planing rules as follows:

1 Choose the *face side* and plane it flat. Check for flatness with a steel rule. When correct mark with a *face side mark* pointing to the face edge (ie the best edge).
2 Plane the *face edge* flat and square. Check for flatness with a steel rule and squareness with a try square. When correct mark with a *face edge mark* pointing to the face side.
3 Gauge to *width* from the face edge. Plane to width. Check for flatness and squareness.
4 Gauge to *thickness* from the face side. Plane to thickness. Check for flatness.

Planing end grain is not as easy as side grain. If the plane is taken straight across, then splitting will occur at the end of the cut (fig 20). One way to avoid this is to cramp a piece of waste wood tightly to the end of the work; then splitting occurs only

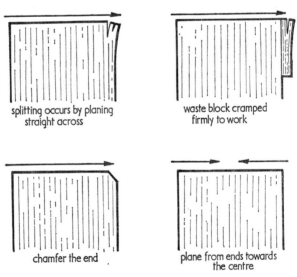

splitting occurs by planing
straight across

waste block cramped
firmly to work

chamfer the end

plane from ends towards
the centre

Fig 20 Methods of planing end grain

in the waste piece. Another method is to remove the far corner of the wood at an angle of 45°. This prevents splitting, but can be done only if the cut corner of the wood will not show because later shaping of the work will remove the cut. The usual method to adopt for planing the end grain of a wide board is to plane half-way from each end.

To plane the end grain of a small piece of wood requires the use of a simple appliance called a shooting board. This device helps one plane a straight square surface. The letters in figure 21 show the purpose of the parts more clearly.

- A This block is put in the vice to hold the shooting board securely.
- B Is the surface which the plane moves along.
- C Is the stock which helps to hold the work square to the plane. The stock has to be at right angles to B.
- D Is a piece of wood which rests in the well of the bench and helps to hold the shooting board in place.
- E Is where the work is rested and held in place against the stock.

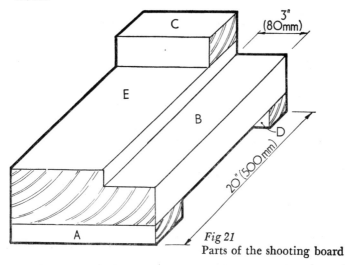

Fig 21
Parts of the shooting board

☐ MALLET

The mallet is made from beechwood, which is hardwearing and does not split easily. It is used chiefly for hitting chisels when working on top of the bench. The usual size for a mallet

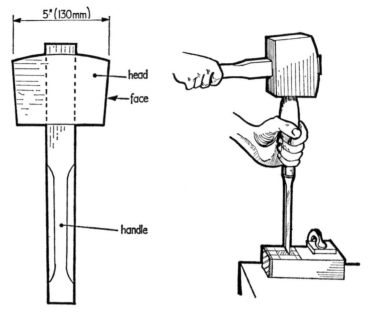

Fig 22 Parts of the mallet *(left)* and using the mallet *(right)*. The face of the mallet is angled so that it hits the chisel squarely

is 5in (130mm) which is measured as in figure 22. The faces are angled so that they always hit the chisel squarely. If they were not angled then the elbow would have to be lifted to an awkward position every time the tool is used. The handle of the mallet is tapered to hold the head in place. Using the mallet forces the head tighter on the shaft.

□ WARRINGTON HAMMER

The warrington hammer has a head of crucible cast steel and a handle made from either ash or hickory. These woods are springy and pass few shocks into the hand. The head is fastened to the handle by one wooden wedge of hornbeam (fig 23) and two malleable iron wedges that are barbed to hold them in place. Should the head become loose on the handle then the metal wedges can be tapped further into the eye of the hammer. The pein of the hammer can be used for tapping small nails which are held upright between the fingers.

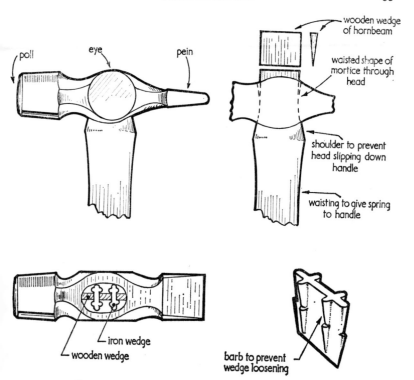

Fig 23 Parts of the warrington hammer. One wooden wedge of hornbeam and two iron wedges are used to fix the hammer head to the shaft

Chapter 2

Saws, Chisels and Planes

HANDSAWS

Wood consists of a mass of closely packed fibres all running in the same direction. These patterns made by the fibres are called the grain of the wood. The handsaw cuts by making a channel either through the grain or across the grain and the wood that is removed from the channel becomes sawdust. The rip saw is designed to cut with the grain. The crosscut saw is designed to cut across the grain.

These saws have three major differences as shown in figure 24. Firstly, the rip saw is longer. It is therefore the faster cuting saw, as longer strokes can be used. Secondly, the teeth of the rip saw are sharpened like chisels, whereas the teeth of the crosscut saw are sharpened like knives. The rip saw can chisel a path through the fibres of the wood. The crosscut saw has to cut across the fibres; it makes two parallel cuts close together so that the wood between these cuts crumbles away. The third difference is that the rip saw has bigger teeth. The size of the teeth is measured as the number of points per inch (per 25mm) or ppi. Alternatively the number of teeth per inch, tpi, can be measured. It will be realised that there is one more point per inch than there are teeth per inch as both outside points are counted. An easy way to recognise the rip saw from the crosscut is to remember that the rip saw has bigger teeth.

Figure 24 also shows that the teeth on both saws are bent outwards alternately. This is called the set of the saw and provides clearance for the blade to pass through the saw cut. Without set the path cut by the saw would be the same width as the thickness of steel in the blade. The saw would then bind in the cut and be difficult to use. A well set saw makes it possible to slide a sewing needle between the teeth of the upturned saw from heel to toe. Best quality saws are taper ground. That is to say the steel blade is thinner at the back than along the roots of the teeth. This way clearance can be provided for the

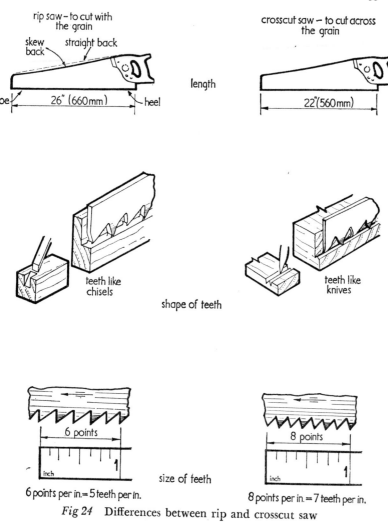

rip saw – to cut with
the grain

skew back   straight back

toe   26" (660mm)   heel

length

crosscut saw – to cut across
the grain

22"(560mm)

teeth like
chisels

shape of teeth

teeth like
knives

6 points

inch   1

6 points per in.= 5 teeth per in.

size of teeth

8 points

inch   1

8 points per in.= 7 teeth per in.

Fig 24   Differences between rip and crosscut saw

saw with less set. The saw cut is therefore narrower and less
work has to be done by the craftsman to achieve the same
results.

Of the tools listed in Appendix A a crosscut saw is recommended since it is the only type of saw that can cut both with
and across the grain. However, cutting with the grain is slower
by crosscut saw than rip saw.

When choosing a new saw check that the teeth are sharp, uniform in shape, and evenly set. Check also the tension of the blade. The saw blade does not stay straight of its own accord. It is tensioned like a spring, by hammer blows placed skilfully along the blade. This work is carried out in the factory by a craftsman. The blade of a good quality saw can be bent so that the toe touches the heel. It should bend in a uniform curve and spring back straight when released.

Fig 25 Crosscutting a plank. The thumb of the left hand guides the blade as the saw is drawn backwards three times

The sawing stool, sometimes called a trestle or horse, is used to support a plank when sawing with a handsaw. Lines to be followed are marked on the work with a pencil giving a generous allowance to the sizes to allow for planing at a later stage. Use two stools to support long work, then the board is held in a horizontal position. The stools must be of sufficient height to prevent the toe of the handsaw striking the floor. A height of about 22in (550mm) is adequate.

Figure 25 shows how a shorter piece of wood may be placed on the sawing stool for sawing. Notice also how the saw is held. Three fingers pass through the handle and the forefinger points alongside in the direction of the cut. This grip is more positive than passing all the fingers through the handle. The work is held firm by placing the left knee on the wood. To commence sawing draw the saw backwards for three strokes guiding the saw by the thumb of the left hand. These three strokes will make a groove on the corner of the wood. This groove acts as a guide for the saw and a forward stroke can be made as soon as the groove is of a reasonable size. Take care with the first few strokes as it is these that determine the accuracy of the cut in regard to the line. Remember that the teeth of the saw are sharpened from toe to heel. Use all the teeth of the saw by making long strokes. Using only the teeth in the middle of the blade will cause them to blunt rapidly. Complete the saw cut by holding the overhanging part and sawing more slowly. Letting the wood fall to the ground can cause a split to run into the work.

BACKED SAWS

Backed saws are so called because the thin blade of the saw is weighted and stiffened by a back of brass or steel. It has been mentioned that the blade of the handsaw is stiffened by skilfully placed hammer blows. The back saw has a thinner and narrower blade and cannot be tensioned in the same way.

The back of the saw is a strip of brass or steel folded tightly over the blade. To tension the blade the back is tapped lightly with one blow of the hammer at point A and again at point B. The natural tendency is for the back to straighten, pulling at the blade at the same time. This pulling action tensions the blade. Best quality backed saws are usually backed with brass, which grips more firmly than steel.

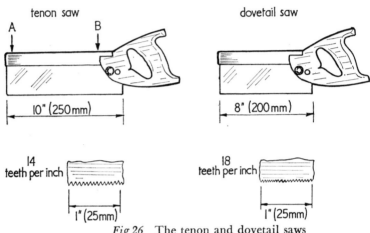

Fig 26   The tenon and dovetail saws

There are two types of backed saws (fig 26). These are the tenon saw and dovetail saw. The main difference is in the length of blade and size of teeth. It has been mentioned that the tenon saw is 10in (250mm) long and has 14 teeth per inch. It is used for accurate bench work. The dovetail saw is only 8in (200mm) long and has 18 teeth per inch. It is used for very fine work, in particular for cutting the dovetail joint. The tenon saw is the most used. Its teeth are relatively large and easy to sharpen. The dovetail saw is reserved for the finer work as its teeth are small and tedious to sharpen.

FRAME SAWS

The majority of work can be undertaken using the saws already mentioned. All straight cuts can be performed by the handsaw or backed saw. However, not all sawing is limited to straight cuts. There are two saws used to cut most curves: the bow saw and coping saw (fig 27). These are sometimes referred to as frame saws because a frame of wood or steel keeps the thin blades taut.

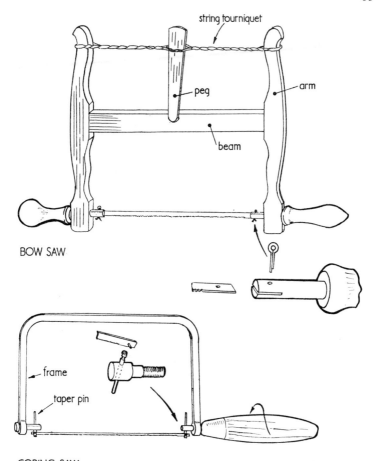

BOW SAW

COPING SAW

Fig 27 Frame saws. The bow saw has a blade length of 10in or 12in (250mm or 300mm) and is used for cutting curves in thick wood. The blade of the coping saw is 6½in (165mm) long. The coping saw is used on thinner wood

The frame of the bow saw is made of beechwood. It consists of two arms loosely jointed to a beam. At one side of the beam there is a loop of string, in the centre of which is a peg. When the peg is turned the string is twisted and thereby shortened. It acts as a tourniquet, the arms being pulled closer together. At the other side of the beam the arms are forced apart. The blade is fastened that side so the action of the tourniquet is to pull the blade taut. When sufficient tension has been applied to the blade, the peg of the tourniquet is rested against the beam to prevent the string unravelling. The blade of the bow saw is supplied with a hole at each end and is fastened to the handles by a small pin. If the pin is lost a small nail with the end bent over can be used.

The coping saw is similar to the bow saw in only a few ways. The frame of the coping saw is made from steel and it is the spring in the frame that keeps the blade taut. The blade is fitted by partly unscrewing the handle, thereby bringing the taper pins closer together. A pin fitted at each end is slipped over the taper pin to hold the blade in place. The handle is then tightened to its full extent. The blade will not break while the handle is being tightened as the frame will spring.

The frame saw cuts a curved path because the narrow blade can be made to turn in the saw cut. Because both hands must be used to grip the handle of the saw, the work is most easily supported in the vice.

On both types of frame saw the blade can be turned inside the frame to cut in any direction. This can be helpful when sawing a long cut near to the edge of a plank. Whilst the blade can be turned every care must be taken not to twist it or a break will occur. Generally the craftsman prefers to have the teeth pointing away from the main handle. The cut is therefore made on the push stroke. This way the sawdust and rough edges do not conceal the line that is being followed. In schools, however, it is quite usual to have the teeth facing towards the handle. The saw then cuts on the pull stroke so the blade is less likely to buckle and be broken. The teeth of frame saws are never sharpened. The blades are cheap and easily replaced.

Frame saws can be used to make an enclosed cut. This is done by drilling a hole in the waste part of the wood and threading the blade through the hole. The blade is fixed to the frame and the shape is sawn. This is only possible when the frame is in reach of the cut.

SPECIAL SAWS

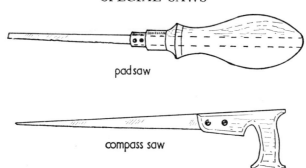

pad saw

compass saw

Fig 28 Special saws. The pad saw *(top)* has a blade length of 8-10in (200-250mm). The compass saw *(bottom)*

These saws are particularly useful when cutting a hole in the middle of a large panel. In this instance work can begin from a drilled hole. The padsaw is slow and it is difficult to keep the blade straight. It is therefore convenient to have only sufficient blade showing. The rest of the blade slides inside the hollow handle. The blade of the padsaw is replaceable and not worth sharpening when blunt. The compass saw would be used for curves of larger radius than the padsaw.

CHISELS

One type of chisel has been mentioned already—the firmer chisel. Sketch (a) represents the $\frac{5}{8}$in (16mm) firmer chisel, and sketch (b) represents the 1in (25mm) firmer chisel. Both sizes are recommended in the tool list given in Appendix A. Notice that the handles are the same size. This is because despite the size of blade the handle must fit the hand. Sketch (c) shows a 1in (25mm) bevelled edge chisel. It looks as though it is sharpened on three edges but there is in fact only one cutting edge. The long edges are not sharp. The bevelled edge chisel is very similar to the firmer chisel. If one imagines the blade of the firmer chisel divided into three equal parts then the bevelled edge chisel is formed by grinding away the outside thirds to form a slope leaving only the centre section flat. Figure 30

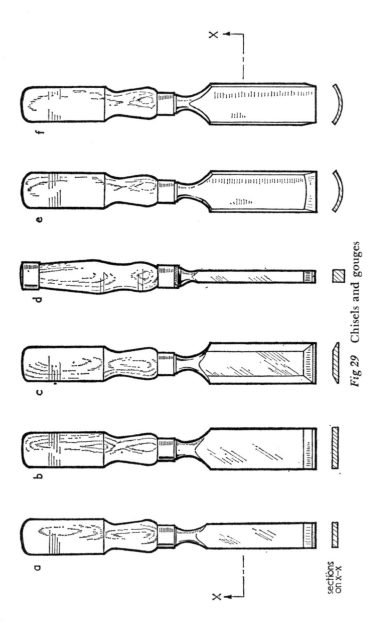

X

X

sections
on x–x

Fig 29 Chisels and gouges

shows the bevelled edge chisel being used to cut away the centre section between two dovetails. The bevels on the chisel allow the tool to work into the undercut corners. This would be an impossible job for the firmer chisel.

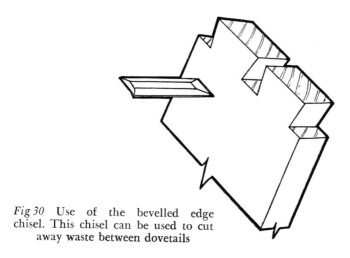

Fig 30 Use of the bevelled edge chisel. This chisel can be used to cut away waste between dovetails

Sketch (d) shows a mortise chisel. It will be noticed that the blade is nearly square in section, and therefore very strong. Sketches (e) and (f) show a tool called a gouge. If one imagines the blade of a firmer chisel heated to red heat and then bent one can see how the gouge is formed. Thinking of a firmer chisel, it is possible to curve the blade in two different ways. Sketch (e) shows the gouge with the sharpening bevel on the inside. This is called the scribing or in-cannel gouge. Sketch (f) shows the gouge with the sharpening bevel on the outside, and this is called the firmer or out-cannel gouge. The firmer gouge is used for hollowing out to make dishes and bowls, whereas the scribing gouge is used for the vertical paring of internal curves.

Figure 31 shows the main parts of the firmer chisel. The blade is fastened to the handle by means of a tang. The tang and the blade are all one piece of tool steel. The tang is a spike forced into the chisel handle. The shoulder prevents the tang from driving up inside the handle when the chisel is struck with a mallet. The ferrule is a seamless brass ring pushed on

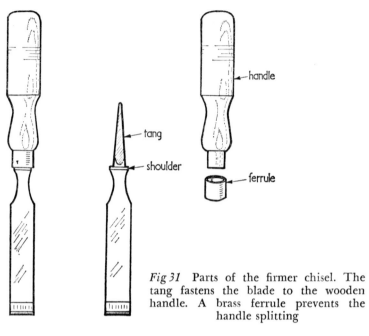

Fig 31 Parts of the firmer chisel. The tang fastens the blade to the wooden handle. A brass ferrule prevents the handle splitting

the handle and held in place by a punch mark. The ferrule prevents the handle from being split by the tang, especially when a new handle is fitted. The bevelled edge chisel is similar to the firmer chisel but it is not as strong and should not be hit heavily with a mallet.

The mortise chisel is rather different. It has a leather washer fitted between the shoulder and the handle to absorb some of the shock to the hand, as this chisel is always used in conjunction with a mallet. Some patterns have a ferrule at the top of the handle to prevent splitting after repeated blows of the mallet. It will be seen that it is not the ferrule that is hit with the mallet but the wood inside the ferrule. The beechwood mallet is never used against metal. Modern chisels have plastic handles. These are very strong and may be hit with a mallet. The advantage of the wooden handle is that it will absorb perspiration.

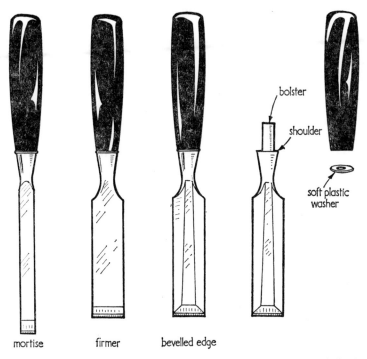

mortise   firmer   bevelled edge

Fig 32 Stanley range of chisels. The mortise, firmer and bevelled edge chisels have handles made of tough plastic. A bolster type construction is used to fasten the handle to the blade

BENCH PLANES

Two planes that have been mentioned previously are the wooden and metal jack planes. All planes have three things in common. Firstly, they each have a cutter. Secondly, they each have a device for holding the cutter in position. In the case of the wooden jack plane it is a wedge; the metal jack plane has a lever cap. The third feature of all planes is the stock or body. This is simply a device used to present the chisel-like blade in a controlled manner to the surface of the wood. Beechwood is used for the stock of the wooden plane because it is a stable and hard wearing timber. The body of the metal plane is made from cast iron.

To remove the cutter of the metal plane lift the lever; this loosens the cap and allows it to be removed, enabling the cutter to be lifted out of the plane. Above the toe of the wooden plane is a small piece of boxwood. This is partly let into the body and is called the button, presumably because of its similarity in shape to the wooden buttons worn on coats years ago. To release the wedge of the wooden plane the stock is held in the hand while the button is tapped two or three times with the hammer. The vibration of the stock causes the wedge to shake out of place. Once the wedge has been removed the cutter can be taken out.

It will be seen that the cutter consists of two parts, the blade and the curling iron (fig 33). The two are held together by a large screw. A large cabinet screwdriver is required to undo this screw but special care must be taken. It is dangerous to hold the blades in the hand while applying pressure with the screwdriver. A slip could cause a bad cut. Instead, place the blades on the bench. Release the screw one turn. It is not necessary to remove the screw entirely as the cutting iron may be slid back from the cutting edge until the screw head can pass through the hole in the blade.

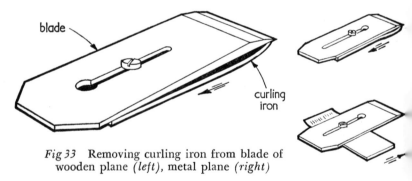

blade

curling iron

Fig 33   Removing curling iron from blade of wooden plane *(left)*, metal plane *(right)*

When removing a cutter from a metal plane greater care is required, as the release hole in the blade is near to the cutting edge. In this instance slacken the screw one turn with the screwdriver. Do not use the lever cap although it seems an ideal fit; the metal is not specially hardened and tempered to act as a screwdriver. Slide the curling iron back from the cutting edge, then swivel the curling iron through 90°. It may now be removed from the blade by sliding forward without the risk of damaging the cutting edge.

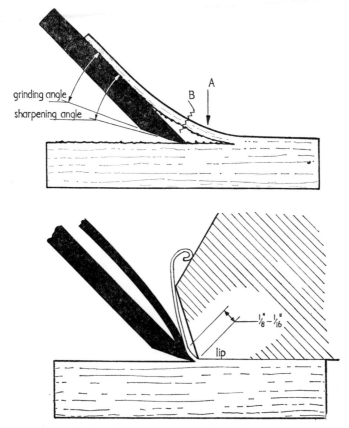

Fig 34   Tearing occurs with single iron

A blade on its own may be tapped into a block of wood with a hammer but splitting occurs ahead of the cutting edge (fig 34) because the blade is acting like a wedge and prising the wood away. This results in a rough surface. Three things can be done to prevent splitting. Firstly, the surface of the wood must be pressed down immediately in front of the cutter to prevent the shaving lifting (*A* fig 34). Pressure is applied by the lip of the plane. Secondly, if the shaving were broken at *B* then it would be prevented from rising up the blade forcing the wood to tear up in front of the cutting edge. This is done by the addition of the curling iron placed about $\frac{1}{8}$in (3mm) from the cutting edge for coarse work and as close to the cutting edge as is practicable for fine work. Thirdly, only fine shavings can be broken by the curling iron so the cutter is set to protrude only a small amount.

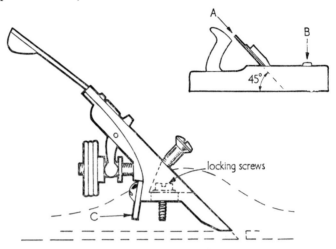

Fig 35   Frogs of wooden and metal planes. The cutter of the wooden plane is adjusted forward by tapping at A and backward by tapping the button B. The depth of cut of the metal plane is adjusted with a knurled knob and lateral adjustment is by means of a lever. Further, the frog of the metal plane may be moved to adjust the size of mouth

The blade of the plane is seated on a part called the frog at an angle of 45° to the sole. This angle is called the pitch of the plane. In the case of the wooden plane the cutter and curling iron are placed on the frog, the wedge pushed in place and the blade is set by tapping at *A* (fig 35) for a coarser shaving or at *B* for a finer shaving. Set also for evenness of cut by tapping the blade sideways. Finally secure the blade by tapping the wedge. Figure 36 shows how to check for cutter projection by holding the plane sole upwards with the light coming from behind the plane. One can then sight along the sole.

The frog of the metal plane is cast as a separate piece from the stock. It is fastened to the stock by two locking screws (fig

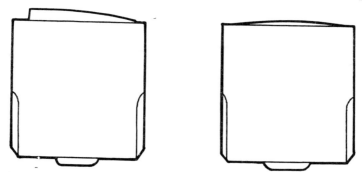

Fig 36 Sighting wooden plane for cutter projection: *(left)* too coarse and uneven; *(right)* correct

35). It will be noticed that the locking screws pass through slots in the frog, and that a lug (*C* fig 35) locates on an adjusting screw on the stock. The principle is that the two locking screws are released one turn and the frog adjusting screw revolved to move the frog forward or back, thereby opening or closing the mouth of the plane. Close the mouth for timbers that are inclined to tear; open the mouth to take coarse shavings and for general purpose work. Should shavings choke in the mouth of the plane do not try to push them through with a steel rule. Remove the lever cap and blade to release the shaving. Choking can indicate that the opening of the mouth is too small or that too coarse a cut is being attempted. Occasionally the edge of the curling iron may be seated incorrectly. This can be remedied by careful use of a file on the curling iron. To alter the amount of cut on the metal plane the knurled adjusting screw must be turned. To set for an even cut the lateral adjustment lever is moved towards one side.

Figure 38 shows the three common metal planes. Each, because of its length, does a particular job best. The smoothing plane, being short, is light, handy and comfortable to work. As its name implies, it is used for finishing off where smoothness is more essential than flatness. It is the plane that is used before the polishing stage of the work. The jack plane is the jack-of-all-trades. It is a general purpose plane. It is used for planing wood to size, trueing edges, and planing ends square on the shooting board. It is long enough to be accurate but light enough to be in use for a long time. The trying plane is

D

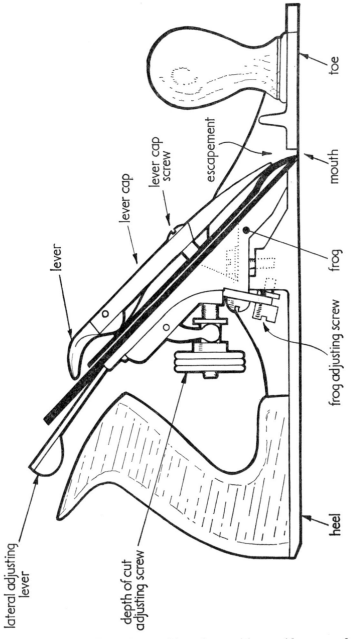

lever cap

lever

lever cap screw

escapement

toe

mouth

frog

frog adjusting screw

lateral adjusting lever

depth of cut adjusting screw

heel

Fig 37 Elevation of metal smoothing plane, with one side removed

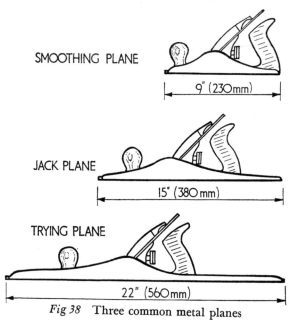

SMOOTHING PLANE

9" (230mm)

JACK PLANE

15" (380 mm)

TRYING PLANE

22" (560mm)

Fig 38 Three common metal planes

about 22in (560mm) long. It is used for trueing long surfaces, and particularly for edge jointing. Its length allows it to ride over minor undulations and take the crests off bumps, thereby achieving a flat surface. This plane should be set to take off only a very fine shaving.

All the metal planes have wooden counterparts. The relative advantages of the wooden and metal planes may be summed up as follows:

Wood	*Metal*
1 Runs more easily over the wood	The sole is machined true
2 The body is robust and more likely to withstand rough treatment	It is less liable to wear
3 Lighter and less tiring to use	The cutting iron is more easily adjusted
4 It is cheaper	The size of the mouth may be adjusted by moving the frog

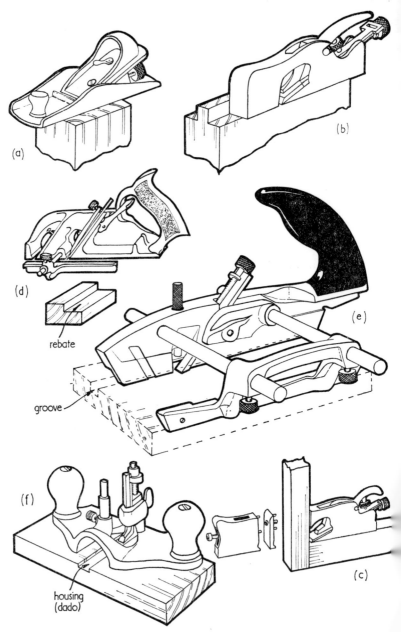

Fig 39 Special planes: (*a*) block plane, (*b*) shoulder plane, (*c*) shoulder/bullnose/chisel plane, (*d*) rebate (rabbet) plane, (*e*) plough plane and (*f*) router

It is recommended in the tool list given in Appendix A that chiefly metal planes are acquired because easy adjustment is a considerable advantage to the beginner. Using the wooden jack plane to plane wood down to size is now largely an anachronism as timber can be easily acquired planed to size by machine. The metal plane is however required to remove the ripple marks left on the wood by machine planing. Many of today's timbers have difficult grains requiring the use of a finely set plane.

All planes work much better if the sole is wiped with a pad moistened with light machine oil. A little linseed oil well rubbed into the stock of the wooden plane serves to preserve the wood.

SPECIAL PLANES

There are several planes that have not yet been mentioned because they have special purposes. The small block plane (fig 39a) may be worked single-handed. It is used chiefly for small work and for trimming end grain. The original function of this plane was to trim the surfaces of butchers blocks, which were made of hardwood with the end grain upwards. This tool has a single blade set into the body of the plane at a shallow angle, bevel uppermost. Owing to its handy size and its efficiency for planing end grain the block plane has been adopted not only by the cabinet maker, but by the model maker as well. It has also been found an exceedingly handy tool for trimming plastic laminates, though in this case the tool works better if it has a low angle of pitch.

The shoulder plane (fig 39b) is used chiefly for trimming shoulders, tenons and rebates. The blade cuts the full width of the body so that this tool can trim right into the angle of the corner. This plane is obtainable with a detachable front section for use as a bullnose plane (fig 39c). As such it may be used to trim right into corners.

The rebate, or rabbet plane (fig 39d), is used to cut a rebate on the corner of a piece of wood. This plane has two fences. One is a stop for cutting the correct depth and the other is a guide for cutting the correct width. These are easily adjusted

to suit the size of rebate required. There are two blade positions. The centre position is used for all normal open-ended
rebating. The forward position is used for bullnose work
when cutting stopped rebates. The blade cuts bevel downwards and adjustment is made with the lever behind the
blade. As there is no curling iron work must begin in progressive stages to minimise tearing of the grain. Start from the
front end by making a short cut and work backwards until the
entire rebate is made.

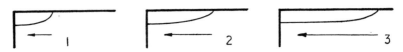

Fig 40   Working a rebate in progressive stages

The plough plane (fig 39e) is used to make a groove inside
the boundaries of the wood but it can also work a rebate. This
plane is supplied with a set of cutters of different widths. A
cutter is chosen to match the width of the groove required.
The plane is then set for depth of the work. As with the rebate
plane, start work at the far end and move backwards gradually. Clear shavings from the mouth of the plane frequently
as it quickly becomes choked. The most common fault when
working with this plane is not holding the fence tightly to the
work. Remember to press inwards with the left hand when
cutting. This requires a little practice but is easily mastered.
A spot of oil on the fence and sole of the plane eases the effort
required.

Figure 41 shows the plough plane being used. Grooving the
edge of a wide board is easy as the wood may be held in the
vice. Often, however, the groove is required in the side of the
work. The wood is then best placed in a sash cramp and the
cramp held in the vice. Always allow the wood to overhang
the vice as part of the plough plane is likely to work below the
wood. The most common trouble is caused by the plane rubbing on the vice.

The router (fig 39f) is used for making grooves of uniform
depth across the grain. A groove cut across the grain is called
a housing or dado (pronounced *day'doe*). The sides of the

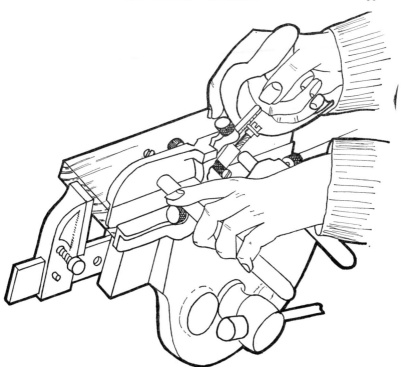

Fig 41 Using a plough plane. The work can be supported in a sash cramp and the sash cramp held in the vice

housing are cut first with the tenon saw and most of the waste is removed with a chisel before the router is used. The router is worked from the edge of the wood towards the centre to avoid splitting. The depth is gradually increased if necessary until the required depth is reached.

The replaceable blade plane (fig 42) is the latest development in plane design. The replaceable blades are made of tungsten steel and are sharpened in the factory ready for use. Three shapes of blade are available. The curved blade is for general planing, the straight blade for rebate work and edge and end grain planing, and a special blade is available for planing hard laminated plastics and manufactured boards such as Formica and chipboard.

A blunt or chipped blade may be easily replaced by slackening the blade clamping screw and allowing the old blade to

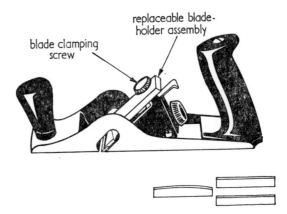

Fig 42 Replaceable blade plane. No sharpening is required because the worn out blades are simply discarded

drop out of the assembly. The plane is then held sole upwards and a new blade slipped in place. Care must be taken to position the blade bevel upwards and to seat the blade squarely in the blade holder assembly. While the plane is still in the inverted position, the blade clamping screw is retightened. The blade can be adjusted for depth of cut and lateral alignment in the usual way. A fence is available and can be used in conjunction with a straight blade to convert the ordinary plane into a rebate plane.

The advantages of the replaceable blade plane are lightness and ease of use. The plane is 10in (250mm) long and has a 2in (51mm) cut. No sharpening is required as the worn out blades are simply discarded.

Chapter 3

Other Hand Tools

MARKING TOOLS

☐ MORTISE GAUGE

The mortise gauge is similar in appearance to the marking gauge, the chief difference being that the mortise gauge has two spurs. This tool is used to mark two lines on the wood parallel to an edge and with the grain. Its use is marking guide lines to be followed with the saw and chisel when cutting the mortise and tenon joint; hence its name.

The distance between the spurs may be varied by adjusting

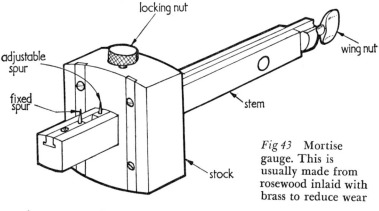

locking nut

wing nut

adjustable spur

fixed spur

stem

stock

Fig 43 Mortise gauge. This is usually made from rosewood inlaid with brass to reduce wear

a wing nut on the end of the stem. The position of the lines from the edge of the work may be adjusted by moving the stock. The stock can be locked by turning the nut provided. It is usual to set the spurs of the mortise gauge to suit the chisel to be used when cutting the mortise, rather than to a set measurement. When the gauge is set correctly the mortise chisel just rests between the points of the spurs.

☐ CUTTING GAUGE

The cutting gauge is used to mark a line on the wood *across* the grain. This tool is similar to the marking gauge but the spur is replaced by a small knife held in place by a brass wedge. The end of the wood must be square and true before this gauge can be used with accuracy.

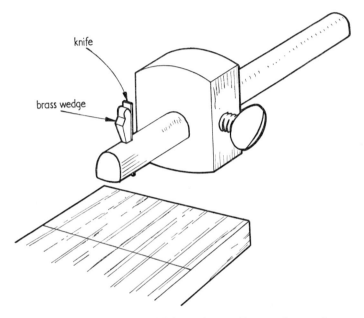

Fig 44   Cutting gauge. This marks one line on the wood across the grain

TESTING TOOLS

☐   MITRE SQUARE

The mitre square is similar to a try square, the difference being that the blade is inclined at an angle of 45° to the stock. It is used therefore for marking out and checking angles of 45° and 135°.

☐   SLIDING BEVEL

The sliding bevel is used for transferring angles other than 45° or 90°. The angle of the blade is adjustable and is locked in place either by a wing nut or a set screw.

It is usual for the angle required to be given not in the

numbers of degrees but as a ratio, in a method similar to that used for informing motorists about the gradient of a hill. Suppose the sliding bevel is to be set to a slope of 1 in 14. It is first necessary to choose a setting out board with one straight

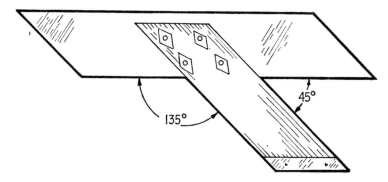

Fig 45   Mitre square. Used for checking the mitre angle of work such as picture frames

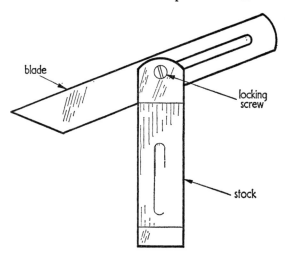

Fig 46   Sliding bevel. Used for transferring angles to the work of other than 90° or 45°

edge; the top of the bench may be used provided it is in good order. Mark a line at right angles to the edge of the board with a pencil and try square. Now it will probably be impracticable to measure along this line a distance of 14in; it will be more convenient if the numbers in the ratio are divided by 2. This will not change the amount of slope. Measure 7in (140mm) along the line from the edge and $\frac{1}{2}$in (10mm) from that point parallel to the edge. Join the positions with a pencil line and set the sliding bevel to this line (fig 47).

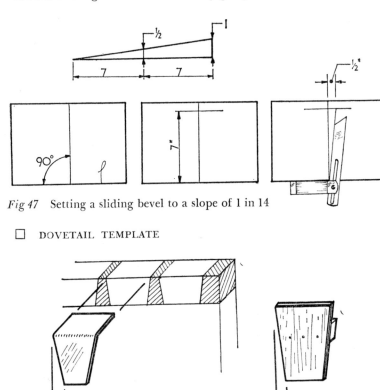

Fig 47 Setting a sliding bevel to a slope of 1 in 14

☐ DOVETAIL TEMPLATE

Fig 48 Dovetail templates: *(left)* made of metal;
(right) made from wood

The dovetail template is used as a pattern when marking the slope of a dovetail. This device can be made from a piece of steel bent and filed to shape, or a piece of shaped plywood.

□ WINDING STRIPS

Winding strips are two parallel strips of well seasoned wood placed at opposite ends of the work; by sighting across the tops of the strips any wind (twist in the wood) can be easily detected. The best way to correct a twisted piece of wood is to place the work against the bench stop and plane diagonally to remove the high spots.

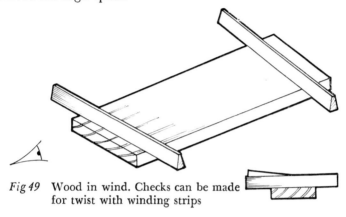

Fig 49   Wood in wind. Checks can be made for twist with winding strips

CUTTING TOOLS

□ CABINET SCRAPER

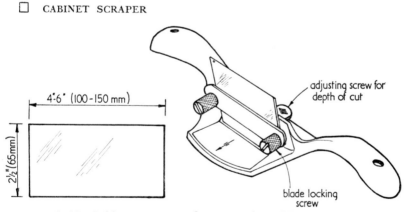

Fig 50   Cabinet scraper and scraper plane. The cabinet scraper has to be sprung in the hands and pushed away from the operator. The scraper plane springs the blade with an adjusting screw and makes the work easier

Some timbers will tear slightly no matter how well the smoothing plane is sharpened and set, and the cabinet scraper may be used to remove these blemishes after the surface has been planed.

The cabinet scraper is used sprung in the hands so make sure the blade is relatively easy to bend. The centre of the convex edge is pushed forward to remove a ribbon of shaving. It is fairly hard work and is best confined to timbers that are difficult to plane. A better surface can generally be achieved with the smoothing plane so it is more worthwhile mastering the skill of the plane than making too frequent use of the scraper. The scraper plane is easier to use than the cabinet scraper as the blade is sprung by a screw instead of pressure from the thumbs. Also the sole of the plane prevents the tool from digging in.

☐   SPOKESHAVE

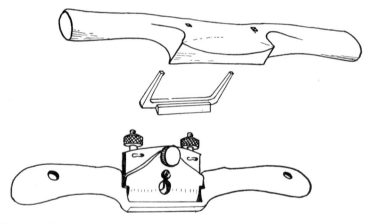

Fig 51   Wooden and metal spokeshave. The metal pattern is available
with a flat or curved sole

The spokeshave was originally used to smooth the spokes of wooden cart wheels and was made of wood with a blade forged by the local blacksmith. Today an all-metal version is available. The wooden spokeshave is made in only one form but there are two types of metal spokeshave: the flat sole spokeshave is used for convex shapes, gentle hollows, and flat cutting; the round sole spokeshave can be used only to make concave shapes.

As well as shaping a curve the spokeshave may be used for smoothing a curve that has been cut to shape with a frame saw. It is possible with this tool to produce a surface which requires no further cleaning up. Care must be taken to always work with the grain.

BORING TOOLS

☐ BRADAWL

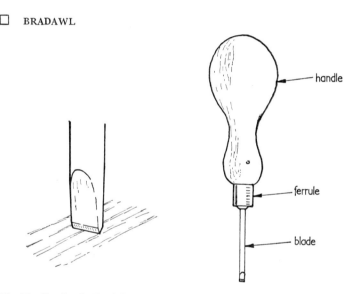

Fig 52 Bradawl. Used for making small holes. Set the blade across the grain and twist and push on the handle

The bradawl is a small chisel-pointed tool used for making holes to start screws. It is used with a semi-rotary action starting with the blade at right-angles to the grain of the wood. The sharp edge of the bradawl cuts the fibres of the wood and the blade pushes the fibres to the sides. A pin through the handle and blade secures the latter and prevents it pulling out from the handle when the bradawl is withdrawn from the work.

☐   HAND DRILL

By far the most satisfactory method of boring small holes in wood is by means of the hand drill. The drill shown in figure 53 has a double pinion drive which is stronger than the less expensive drills with single pinions. The hand drill has a three-jaw chuck which will only accept round-shanked drills. This limits its use to the twist drill and round-shanked countersink. It will grip drills up to at least $\frac{1}{4}$in (6mm) in size.

The point of a drill is rather blunt, and so it is good practice

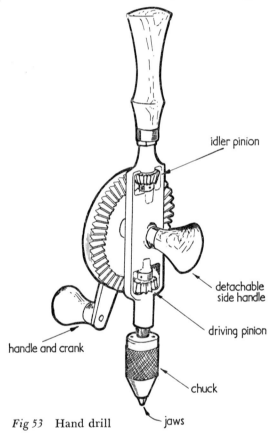

idler pinion

detachable
side handle

driving pinion

handle and crank

chuck

Fig 53 Hand drill   jaws

to locate the required centre of the hole by means of a centre punch. This prevents the tendency of the blunt point to wander from the correct position at the start of drilling.

Hold the drill straight. Do not wobble while turning as it makes the hole oversize and is likely to break the drill. Turn the crank at a constant speed and not too fast. The same rules apply when withdrawing the drill, when there is even greater danger of the drill breaking. Always keep the drill turning in a clockwise direction or the waste will be left in the hole.

☐ TWIST DRILLS

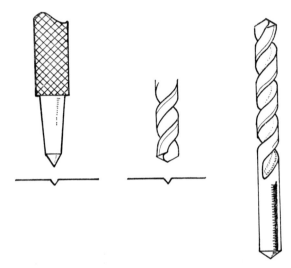

Fig 54 Twist drill and the use of the centre punch to locate the drill

The twist drill is used for making small holes into which screws are fitted. These drills can be bought in sizes from $\frac{1}{16}$in (1.5mm) to $\frac{1}{4}$in (6mm) for use in the hand drill. Larger sizes are obtainable but these require more powerful drilling machines to turn them. Twist drills may be made of carbon tool steel or high-speed steel. The high-speed steel, though more expensive, is the better type as it is stronger and can be used with greater reliability in the electric drill.

When drilling deep holes the twist drill is liable to clog with waste. To prevent this the drill should be withdrawn frequently from the hole and the flutes cleared. The twist drill is sometimes called the Morse drill after the name of the American inventor.

E

☐   BRACE

The bits used for boring large holes require considerable leverage to turn them. The power of the brace is dependent upon the sweep. This tool can be bought with different amounts of sweep. A brace with a large sweep will exert more power on the bit. A useful size is an 8in (200mm) sweep. The head of the brace is fitted with ball bearings so that it may be held steady as the brace is turned. A more expensive brace has a ratchet fitted above the chuck. This enables the brace to be

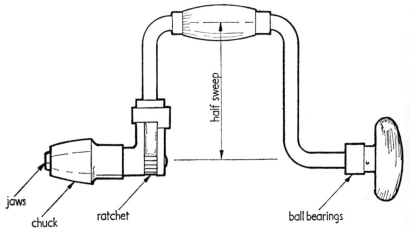

jaws

chuck   ratchet   ball bearings

Fig 55   Brace. Used to bore holes greater than ¼in (6mm) in diameter

used in awkward places, against a wall for instance, where the brace cannot be swung through a complete circle. The chuck of the brace has two jaws that will in general only grip square shank bits. It will not accept the twist drill which should of course be used in a hand drill.

☐   BITS

Figure 56 shows the most common types of bits made to fit the brace. The centre bit is used for cutting a clean hole in thin timber. In operation the brad point is placed onto the centre mark on the work. Turning the brace causes the point to penetrate. The scriber then cuts a circular path through the grain of the wood. Finally the cutter lifts the waste. The bit operates successfully when drilling holes in thin wood but is inclined to wander with the grain when drilling to a good depth.

The Jennings pattern twist bit may be used successfully when deep boring. The spiral twist not only removes the waste from the bottom of the hole, but also the edges of the spiral press against the side of the hole making the bit follow a straight and accurate path. This is the bit most frequently used by the cabinet maker.

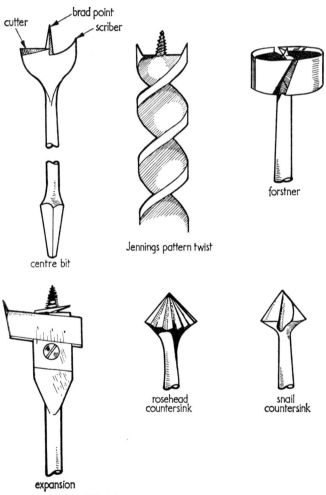

Fig 56 Common types of bit

The Forstner bit is used for drilling holes when an almost flat bottom is required. This bit is rather more specialised than the previous two but sometimes it is invaluable.

All the bits mentioned can be bought in a range of sizes from $\frac{1}{4}$in (6mm) to at least 1in (25mm). It is useful to have a selection of these so that holes in the more common size range can be readily produced. The expansion bit, however, can be adjusted to make holes from $\frac{7}{8}$in (22mm) to 3in (76mm) in diameter.

The countersink bit is used to bore conical holes in hardwood in order that the heads of countersink screws may be fitted flush with the surface of the work. Two types of countersink bit are available. The rose pattern may be used on brass as well as wood. The snail pattern countersink is used for wood alone and provides a slightly better finish.

A useful addition to a range of bits is the turnscrew bit. As its name implies it can adapt the brace for use as a screwdriver. It is so efficient that one has to take care not to apply too much pressure and snap the screw.

When using any bit to drill a hole right through a piece of wood splitting will always occur on the far side of the work unless certain precautions are taken. The simplest way to avoid splitting is to drill through the wood until the point penetrates, then reverse the wood and drill in from the other side. Unfortunately this method will not work when drilling thin wood. In this instance when the point of the bit emerges on the far side of the work it is possible that it has not even started to shape the hole on the near side. To overcome this difficulty place a waste piece of wood directly behind the work and cramp the two firmly together either with a cramp, or by placing them low down in the vice. Drilling through the work into the waste will result in a clean cut hole.

MISCELLANEOUS TOOLS

☐ SCREWDRIVER

There are many patterns of screwdriver. The duties of a cabinet screwdriver involve setting the mortise gauge and sliding bevel, undoing the blade and curling iron of the plane, as

well as turning screws. Some people say this tool is misnamed.
It is argued that the hammer is used to drive nails and the
screwdriver is used to turn screws. Perhaps this tool should
therefore be called a turnscrew.

The handle of the screwdriver is made of beechwood and is
shaped for pushing and turning. The part of the blade that
enters the handle is rectangular to prevent the handle from
turning on the blade. The large handle over a small blade
produces great turning power. Several screwdrivers should be
bought to fit screws of different sizes.

☐ NAIL PUNCH

Fig 57   Nail punch, sometimes called a nail set

The nail punch is used to sink the heads of nails below the
surface of the work. Place the punch on the nail and tap the
head of the punch with a hammer. The resulting hole may
be hidden with filler, such as hard beeswax pressed in with a
bradawl on work that is to be polished, or putty on work that
is to be painted. Two punches are needed, small and large,
and the hollow point pattern are better, being less liable to
jump from the head of the nail.

☐ PINCERS

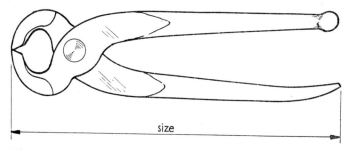

Fig 58   Pincers. Protect the surface of the work by levering on
to a pad of waste wood

Several types of pincers are available and the tower pattern illustrated is the most popular. These may be bought in a range of sizes, the 8in (200mm) size being the most useful. When using the pincers to withdraw a nail it is advisable to place a piece of waste wood between the jaw and the surface of the work. This prevents the jaw from damaging the surface. The claw may be used to withdraw nails from awkward places.

AIDS AND APPLIANCES

☐ MITRE BLOCK

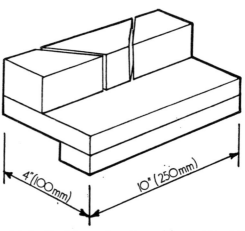

Fig 59   Mitre block. Used in conjunction with a tenon saw for cutting
the ends of small beading to an angle of 45?

The mitre block is similar in appearance to the bench hook, but it is designed specifically to assist with holding the tenon saw at a steady 45° angle to the work. This appliance is seldom sufficiently accurate when working mouldings of large section, so its use is best confined to cutting the mitre corners of small beadings and light picture frames. Made of beechwood and used with care this tool can have a reasonably long life.

☐ MITRE BOX
The mitre box is used to guide the saw at a controlled angle

of 45° to the work. This tool is better than the mitre block as the saw is guided on both sides of the work. This device can be used on mouldings of large section. Accurate mitre joints can be cut straight from the saw if a fine tooth tenon saw is used and the moulding is cut so that the ragged edge is produced on the back of the work.

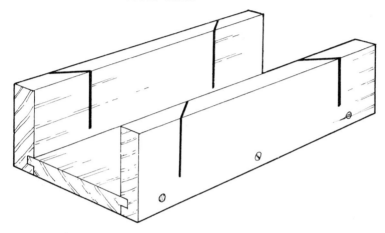

Fig 60   Mitre box. This has similar uses to a mitre block, but is much sturdier and may therefore be used on larger pieces of work. Insert a piece of waste wood inside the box to prevent the saw cutting into the base

☐   MITRE SHOOTING BOARD

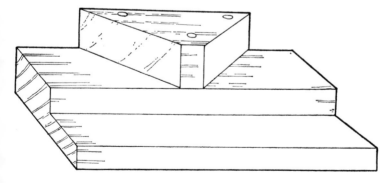

Fig 61   Mitre shooting board. Used for trimming the ends of moulding previously sawn to 45°

This device may be used for trimming the ends of mould-ings cut to shape previously in the mitre box. It is similar in use and appearance to the shooting board. The work may be placed in either of two positions because mouldings can sel-dom be reversed to trim the mitre.

☐   GUILLOTINE

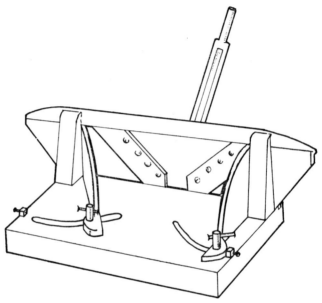

Fig 62   Guillotine. A powerful machine that can be used to trim the ends of wood to any angle between 45° and 90°

The guillotine is a sturdy hand powered cutter used for trimming end grain. With large blades and a long handle it is capable of trimming mouldings of large section. The mould-ing is prepared roughly to the angle by saw then accurately trimmed on the guillotine. Only fine shavings should be re-moved from the work. The angle plates have a range of ad-justment from 45° to 90°.

CRAMPS

☐   G CRAMP

The G cramp is so called because it is in the shape of a letter G. It can be used for holding two pieces of wood together while the glue sets between them, or it can be used to

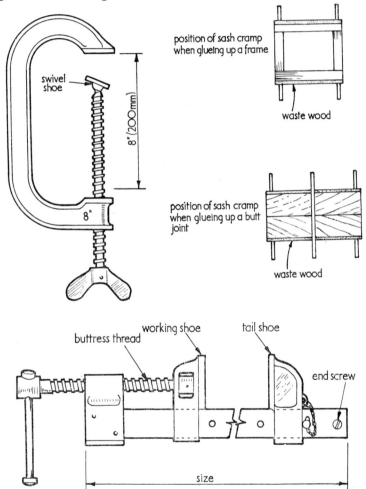

Figs 63 & 64   G cramp *(top left)*. Sash cramp *(right and below)*, showing how to position the cramps when glueing up a frame and a butt joint between boards

hold the work steady on the bench leaving both hands free to work with the tools. A useful size of G cramp is 8in (200mm). One G cramp is essential amongst a kit of tools and a good workshop will have many of different sizes.

☐ SASH CRAMP

The sash cramp is mainly used for holding work together while the glue sets. It has a short thread on the working shoe and main adjustments are made by sliding the tail shoe along the bar. A useful size of sash cramp is 36in (910mm). It is best to buy a pair of cramps because usually two are needed on the work. Always use a piece of waste wood between the shoe of the cramp and the work as this helps to spread the pressure and prevent the shoe from marking the work.

☐ T-BAR CRAMP

The T-bar cramp is similar in appearance to the sash cramp but the section through the bar is in the shape of a letter T. This gives the cramp greater strength and rigidity. It is intended for use on large and heavy work. There are disadvantages in using a cramp that is too big for the job. It can

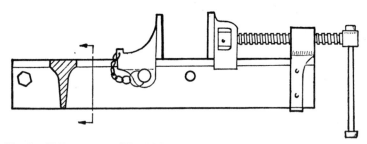

Fig 65   T-Bar cramp. The T-bar section produces a very strong cramp but these cramps are usually too heavy for furniture making

distort the work and one cannot feel how much pressure is being applied.

☐ HANDSCREW

The handscrew is a useful cramp sometimes made entirely of wood but more commonly made with beech chops and

metal screws. To open or close the handscrew grasp the
handles firmly one in each hand and spin the wooden chops
head over heels. In operation arrange the jaws parallel and the
same distance apart as the thickness of the work. Fasten to the
work by tightening screw A and then turn screw B so that the
chops pinch firmly in place.

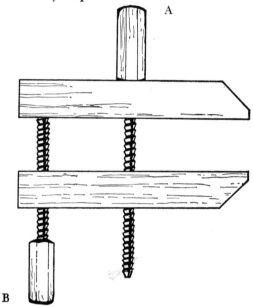

Fig 66   Handscrew. A very useful cramp

Chapter 4

Maintenance of Hand Tools

CARE OF TOOLS

Good tools are expensive and they should be carefully maintained. This will not only avoid the unnecessary expense of premature replacement, it will also mean that the tools are always ready for use. Nothing can be more irksome than having to sharpen or mend tools before work can commence. Probably the most satisfactory method of organising these chores is to perform them as one works, and above all to make sure that the workshop and its equipment are left in good order at the end of the day ready for a prompt start on the next occasion.

Rather like the motor car, servicing of tools depends on the amount of work they are given. A well-used jack plane will require frequent sharpening. Remember, though, that tools left idle for long periods will also require maintenance. The biggest problem is the deterioration of steel tools through rust. A rust-pitted chisel will not sharpen; the face must be reground to a smooth, flat surface and this is very time consuming. There are several ways of preventing the formation of rust. Primarily, the finer the surface finish given to the steel then the greater resistance there will be to rust. Well polished tools as supplied by the manufacturer will help maintain themselves in a good state, but some protection should be given to tools that are to be stored for a period of time or are used only occasionally. Water and air must be excluded from the surface of the metal, and even in the best ventilated workshop moisture can be transferred to the metal by contact with sweaty hands. Petroleum jelly should be applied liberally and thoroughly to form a protective barrier. By wrapping the object in newspaper one can prevent the transfer of petroleum jelly to other things. Grease is a good substitute for petroleum jelly; in fact some people find it more efficient. A vapour barrier paper such as *Banrust* is frequently used by manufacturers to save the time and trouble of greasing their tools in transit. It is of course more convenient for the customer if the tool is not covered with grease. The tool must be placed in an enclosed container with the white side of the paper, which is the treated side, facing the steel parts of the tool. This will ward off rust for lengthy periods of time. One of the latest products for treating steel is *Lubysil 717*. This is sold in 8oz (227g) aerosol cans. The liquid consists of a non soap based grease and mineral oil base containing silicone resins. This has excellent dielectric, corrosion resisting and lubricating properties. Furthermore this liquid is not inflammable. Sprayed on to metal, Lubysil forms a smooth transparent layer with an imperceptible skin, which resists condensation, water, and salt- and sulphur-laden air. Equipment treated this way is ready for use without time spent unpacking and cleaning.

In the same way that steel tools require periodic maintenance, so wooden tools require some preservative treatment. All wooden parts of tools deserve wiping with a rag soaked in linseed oil once a year. This drying oil, made from the exudation of the crushed seeds of the linen (flax) plant, helps preserve the wood and eases the work by reducing friction. Sometimes a little turpentine is added to the oil to make a kind of teak oil. This will impart a little shine to the wood.

Maintenance can be looked at in two ways. There is the more general maintenance of all tools to preserve them and to ensure they work at optimum efficiency, and there is the normal sharpening procedure required for all cutting tools, except of course the replaceable blade plane.

Spare parts are available for all the tools supplied by reputable manufacturers. Make sure that the tool supplier is given the exact serial number of the tool, and full details of the part required.

The following is a list of common hand tools. More specific advice is given here on the maintenance and sharpening of these tools though it is suggested that all tools be looked at in this light at least once a year, and preferably twice a year, say spring and autumn.

□ BENCH

It should be remembered that the bench is as important to

the craftsman as the saw and the plane. The working surface should be protected from saw cuts by a bench hook, and a chiselling board should be used when doing vertical paring or chopping a through mortise.

An occasional inspection for nails and panel pins driven into the bench top will save nasty snags to sharp cutting edges. Any nail that can be withdrawn must be taken out with pincers even at the expense of making a hole in the top of the bench. Use a screwdriver and mallet to cut the wood from around the nail. Pliers can sometimes reach where pincers fail. The most stubborn of nails should be punched well below the surface of the bench.

Despite all one's efforts to protect the top and keep it flat and true, the timber will move in time and gradual wear will take place particularly in the region of the vice. The movement of wood and tools on the surface of the bench will gradually wear a hollow. Placing wood on a hollow bench top for the purposes of planing is obviously not possible. The top must be retrued. For this task there is no better tool than the trying plane. Make sure the plane is sharp and finely set, as beech is hard to work. A little oil on the sole of the plane will ease the work. Plane first across the grain, then diagonally, and finish with the grain. A long steel rule or straight edge will help to check the trueness of the work. Remove the sharp edge around the top of the bench with a few strokes of the plane.

☐ BENCH HOOK

The bench hook will last only a few years. Its purpose, apart from helping to hold the wood when sawing, is to protect the surface of the bench from the teeth of the tenon saw. A new bench hook can be quickly made in the workshop from a hardwood such as beech. Rather than drill and dowel first, it is easier to glue the blocks in place and drill for the dowels after the glue has set. As mentioned in Chapter I it is not good practice to secure the blocks with screws as these can easily damage the teeth of the saw. Try to avoid dropping the bench hook as it will break just like other tools.

☐ BRACE AND BITS

The wooden handles of the brace require only occasional attention. Wiping them over with a rag previously dipped in linseed oil will help preserve the wood. Braces fitted with plastic handles require little maintenance to the plastic other than wiping clean with a damp cloth. The metal frames that are unplated can be polished with wire wool or fine emery cloth dipped in mineral oil. This treatment is not suitable for braces plated with chromium or nickel as it would remove the plating. Plated braces are cleaned and maintained by wiping the frame with an oil soaked rag. Remember to use mineral oil for metal work and linseed oil for wooden parts. The latter, being a vegetable oil, is a drying oil and not suitable for the oiling of metal parts.

The brace will usually benefit from a few drops of oil placed on the ball race under the head. A brace fitted with a plastic head can have the mouldings separated with a penknife, but it is advisable to read the manufacturer's instructions first. A spot of lubricating oil can be placed on the bearing inside the head and the plastic mouldings will snap together with firm pressure. Remember that woodworking tools are kept in a dusty atmosphere and this quickly dries the oil. Consequently it is advisable to oil all moving parts little and often.

Grease applied to the thread of the chuck and a little spread on the inside cone of the chuck will aid smooth operation of the brace. A grease recommended for the workshop is *Lubysil GPI* grease. This is a soft silicone grease and works well in enclosed gearboxes and bearings. Never use a high pressure oil on hand tools as this promotes very rapid wear of the tool. Always try to prevent over oiling or over greasing, which can at the least make things very messy.

Bits for the brace are sharpened with a needle file (fig 67) and occasionally an oilstone is employed to provide that extra keen edge. Various sectional shapes of needle file are obtainable, but chiefly square, triangular, flat, round and half-round files are suitable for our purposes. It is worth obtaining a set of needle files as they have other uses such as sharpening saws (see later in this chapter).

The sharpening of bits consists chiefly of following the

angles already established by the manufacturer. Never touch the outside of the bit with a file or the bit will bore an under-size hole and probably, worse, it will get stuck in the hole being drilled.

A centre bit is sharpened by pushing the point into a spare

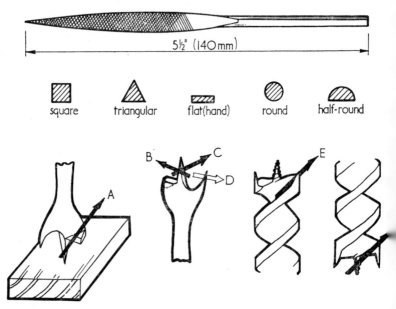

Fig 67 Needle file and sharpening bits for the brace: *(top)* sections through some of the needle files available; *(bottom)* try to follow the bevels already established on the bits and never sharpen on the outside of the bit

piece of wood. The bevel can then be filed until the cutting edge is sharp (fig 67a). The inside of the scriber may be touched with a file (fig 67d), and with the bit upturned the brad point can be sharpened (fig 67 b c). Remember to follow the angles existing on the bit and use the safe edge (non-milled surface) of the file where necessary to prevent damaging an adjoining surface. The sharpening of the twist bit is also detailed in figure 67.

☐ BRADAWL

The bradawl is easy to sharpen if one considers how it

works. The cutting edge should be sharp in order to sever the fibres of the grain, and the gently sloping faces are used to force the fibres outwards. A small metalworking vice is handy for holding small tools, such as the bradawl, while working on them with a file. Such a vice can be conveniently mounted on a wooden block and the block held in the woodworking vice.

☐ CHISELS

It is not easy to say how often a chisel will need to be sharpened as this very much depends on the type of wood being cut. Certain timbers will require that the chisel be sharpened after every six cuts. Other timbers may necessitate sharpening the chisel only every half-hour of use. The beginner is not always sure when a chisel is blunt and may find the following guidance helpful There are four signs used by the craftsman:

1 Inspect the work for the quality of cut
2 Think about the ease with which the chisel performs the desired operation
3 Look to see if the cutting edge is polished with use as this will be seen as a reflection of light from the rounded edge
4 Check the quality of the cutting edge by drawing the tip of the thumbnail across it

An oilstone is used to sharpen the chisel. The oilstone, as its name implies, is oil on stone. The stone may be quarried, in which case it is likely to have come from *Washita* or *Arkansas*, USA, and will be called after its place of origin. Quarried stones are known as natural stones and are expensive, but cheaper artificial stones such as *Carborundum* and *India* make good alternatives. The artificial stones generally belong to one of two types, silicon carbide or aluminium oxide. Both types make excellent stones. Having been produced in an electric furnace these artificial stones have a great consistency in their quality.

Oilstones are generally 8in x 2in x 1in (200mm x 50mm x 25mm). This size is convenient for sharpening plane irons as well as chisels. As the stone is delicate is is usually stored and used in a shallow tray (fig 68 i). At either end of the stone a

F

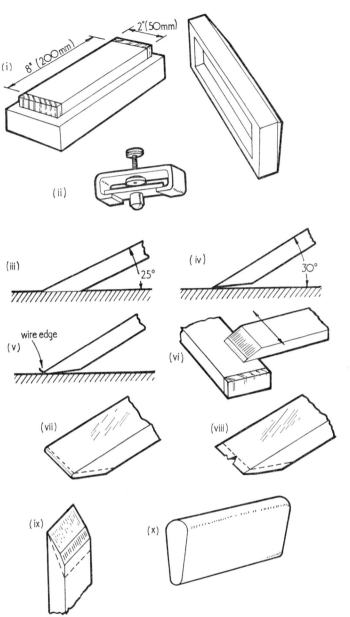

Fig 68 Sharpening a chisel: (*i*) oilstone in case with lid to keep dust off, (*ii*) honing guide to help maintain the correct sharpening angle of 30°, (*iii*) chisel stood on oilstone at 25°, (*iv*) chisel raised to 30°, (*v*) wire edge (burr) turned up by sharpening, (*vi*) place chisel flat on stone to remove wire edge, (*vii*) rounding of edge caused by careless sharpening, (*viii*) gashed edge, (*ix*) chisel with large sharpening bevel is slow to sharpen so requires grinding first, (*x*) oilstone slip used to sharpen gouge

piece of hardwood is fitted end grain uppermost and level with the surface of the stone. This provides a run-off for the tools. It ensures even wear of the stone, allowing the whole surface to be used when sharpening. Only a flat oilstone will sharpen correctly. A hollow stone can be flattened by rubbing on the surface of a sheet of glass using carborundum paste as an abrasive. This is a tedious task and should be avoided. A lid should be provided to keep the stone free from dust.

The surface of the stone is lubricated with neatsfoot oil or thin lubricating oil such as that used for bicycles. Neatsfoot oil is used for softening saddles and leather goods and is usually obtainable from stores specialising in this equipment. A drying oil such as linseed oil would gum up the stone. Such a stone has to be cleaned by soaking in a bath of paraffin. Therefore a non-drying oil must be used: (1) It cleans the stone by washing away the particles of metal. (2) It reduces friction. (3) It cools the edge of the blade. (4) It helps to polish the metal and produce a finer edge.

A new chisel has a grinding bevel of 25°. Chisels are ground to this angle in the factory but, to avoid danger during transit, are not sharpened. From the variety of chisels in the tool kit, it is recommended that the beginner choose a large firmer chisel to practice sharpening.

To sharpen a chisel on the oilstone, first stand the blade on the grinding bevel (fig 68 iii), then lift the blade through 5° to the sharpening angle of 30° (fig 68 iv). Various guides are available to help maintain this angle and can be a great help to the beginner (fig 68 ii). In time one learns to do without these devices, finding the 30° angle as a matter of habit. Push the blade from one end of the stone to the other keeping the angle constant. Avoid rocking the chisel as this will cause the sharpening bevel to be rounded and result in a dulled edge. Sharpen at the 30° angle until a burr, or wire edge, appears on the back of the blade (fig 68 v). This can be felt by sliding the finger down the blade and across the edge. The burr is removed by rubbing the back of the chisel FLAT on the oilstone (fig 68 vi). To remove the burr hold only the blade of the chisel. Bunch the fingers over the cutting edge to provide pressure and polish only the first inch of the blade on the stone, making every effort to keep the blade flat. After a short time the blade will acquire a mirror-like finish. Some crafts-men like to spend time honing the back of every new chisel to this mirror finish. An extra edge can be produced by strop-ping the cutting edge on oiled leather dressed with jewellers' rouge, but this practice is usually restricted to the tools of the woodcarver.

From time to time all chisels, and for that matter plane irons, have to be reground to restore them to the single bevel angle of 25° as supplied by the tool manufacturer. Firstly, careless sharpening may have produced a cutting edge that, while sharp, will not work satisfactorily because it is rounded and rollerskates from the work (fig 68 vii). This may be due to using a hollow stone, or lifting the blade as it is sharpened on the flat side. Secondly, careless use can result in a chipped blade (fig 68 viii). This will leave score marks on the surface of the work. The third reason for grinding results from normal and proper use. A blade that has been sharpened many times acquires a large sharpening bevel (fig 68 ix). This becomes a lengthy task to sharpen on the oilstone. In these three cases the cutters require grinding back to the areas indicated by broken lines. Grindstones are used because they are quick-cutting stones. However, they leave a rough edge on the blade which is unsuitable for cutting wood. The slower-cutting oil-stone is therefore used to achieve the final cutting edge.

Three types of grindstone are in general use. The high-speed dry grinding wheel to be found in most metal working establishments, and often offered as an accessory for the elec-tric drill, is unsuitable for our purpose. It is fast-running and quickly overheats the metal despite frequent quenching in water. All steel tools are specially heat treated. Reheating the steel will remove many of these qualities. A tool damaged in this way will fail to sharpen as it will not retain a cutting edge, and furthermore it is likely to break in use. Such damage can be caused unwittingly in a few seconds by using the high-speed wheel. Breakage can be recognised on the blade as a striated band of colour but when this appears it is too late. Though one can remove the colours from the surface of the metal the damage has been done.

The traditional type of grindstone made from natural grit sandstone is slow-running and powered by an electric motor.

The cutting edge is cooled and the surface of the stone cleaned by water dripped from a tank above the stone. This method of grinding requires a fair amount of skill but it gives a good edge to the tools. The stone should not be left standing in water as it will soften one portion and wear out of shape. These stones can be maintained true and square by occasionally applying the end of an iron pipe across the working surface. All sludge and water from the stone must be drained from the tank after use and tipped on waste ground.

The modern horizontal grindstone is successfully replacing the traditional sandstone. In appearance it is not unlike a large record player. The wheel is artificial and has an extremely long life. Oil is used as a coolant and lubricant, and for washing away the metal swarf. A filter inside the machine traps all the metal particles before the oil is returned in another cycle. An excellent toolrest holds the blade at the chosen angle to the stone and helps one achieve great accuracy.

One of the benefits of attending evening school is that grinding facilities will be available. When working alone one seldom has these facilities. Enquiries then have to be made at the tool shop. Remember, however, that though tools require frequent sharpening they should be infrequently ground as grinding rapidly shortens the life of a tool.

Figure 68 (x) shows an oilstone slip. This is used for sharpening gouges. It is used with oil on the inside of the scribing gouge to sharpen it, the burr being removed on a flat oilstone. The firmer gouge is sharpened in a figure of eight movement on the flat oilstone and the burr removed from the inside of the gouge with the oilstone slip.

□ CRAMPS

Cramps are often used but seldom maintained. Left in a neglected state the cramps are a curse. Moisture left when glueing up causes the bar to rust, glue itself sticks to the bar and the shoes will not slide easily. Cramps not fitted with the Deacon Patent tail slide (a Woden product) can be missing the peg where the chain has snapped.

The bar of the cramp should be regularly cleaned to remove all traces of rust and glue. Polish the bar if necessary with emery cloth and oil. This will help the tail shoe to slide easily with gentle hand pressure. Oil the screw thread. Check the condition of the chain that secures the peg. Replace the chain if necessary. Fit a nut and bolt to the end of the bar to prevent the loose shoe from falling onto the floor and becoming lost in the shavings. New cramps are supplied with a bolt at the end of the bar; if these are removed to extend the cramp, remember to replace them.

□   GAUGES

The three gauges—mortise, marking and cutting—should have the wooden parts wiped with a rag dipped in linseed oil. The metal screw of the mortise gauge will benefit from a few drops of light machine oil. The spurs of the mortise and marking gauges become blunt after a period of use and require sharpening with a file. The cutter of the cutting gauge can be sharpened on a fine oilstone. Some people like a rounded shape whereas others prefer a pointed one. If the shape of the cutter as supplied by the manufacturer suits you, then follow this as closely as possible when sharpening.

□   HAMMER

Everyone knows of the hammer that bends nails. This usually happens when the hammer has a dirty face. Carelessness can result in paint or varnish adhering or glue still covering the face of the hammer after the assembly of a job. Polish the metal parts of the hammer with emery cloth and oil. The pein of the hammer should be made to shine as well as the poll (face end). The handle of the hammer can be rubbed with a linseed-oiled rag and inspected carefully for splits. Test the head for any play and if necessary tap the metal wedge further into the eye.

□   MALLET

The mallet requires very little maintenance. The wood will benefit from a wipe with a linseed oil rag.

□   MARKING KNIFE

The marking knife requires fairly frequent sharpening. It must be able to cut the fibres of the wood cleanly. Some people prefer the knife sharpened on one side like a chisel, but the most popular method is to sharpen the knife with bevels on either side. Penknives are usually sharpened in this fashion and indeed penknives can make excellent marking knives. Push the blade of the knife forward on the oilstone at a low angle. Turn the knife over and pull it back. This way the problems that can be caused by a burr are eliminated. Polish the wooden handle with a linseed oil rag and check the rivets for tightness.

☐ PLANES

Planes, like chisels, require frequent sharpening. The pitch angle of most planes is 45°. If the blade was sharpened at 45° friction would be great because the bevel would rub the surface of the wood (fig 69a). If the blade was sharpened at a low angle (fig 69b) either the edge would snap off or the blade would be bent against the frog until it gained sufficient energy to spring forward. This springing movement, heard as chattering, would result in a poor finish. Practice has shown that a 5° clearance angle is sufficient for a plane (fig 69c). The blade is given plenty of support from the frog and friction is reduced to a minimum. However, sharpening is still a lengthy procedure as a lot of metal has to be removed on the oilstone to gain a new edge. Most of the metal is therefore removed first on the grindstone, and the final edge is given to the cutter on the oilstone. The grinding angle is about 25° and the sharpening angle about 30°. This gives a clearance angle of about 5°, but as many people sharpen at an angle a little greater than the 30° angle normally recommended, then the clearance angle usually lies somewhere between 5° and 15°. In the case of the bench plane never sharpen the iron at an angle greater than the pitch angle of the plane.

The method of sharpening planes and chisels can be considered identical except for one important factor: the profile shape of the plane blade has to vary with the function of the plane. The blades of the rebate and plough planes are sharpened straight and square (fig 69d). It is not easy for the beginner to achieve this shape. It requires care and practice. The cutters of the plough plane are usually ground by the manufacturers to an angle of 35° and the manufacturers recommend that these cutters are sharpened on their grinding bevel.

The block, smoothing and trying planes are sharpened similar to the rebate plane but the corners of the cutting edges are rounded off on the oilstone to prevent the cutter digging in and scoring the work (fig 69e). The jack plane has a cutting

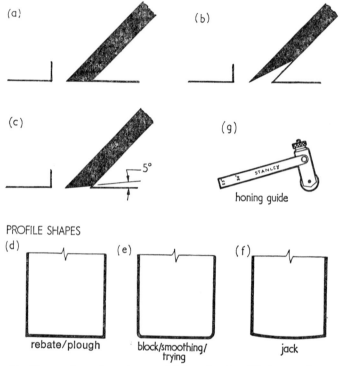

Fig 69 Sharpening plane irons: (*a*) bevel rubs, (*b*) sharpening angle too acute causing chattering, (*c*) 5° clearance angle is sufficient, (*d*) (*e*) (*f*) profile shape of cutters and (*g*) honing guide

edge that is rounded in profile so it may be used to remove coarse shavings (fig 69f). When planing wood from the rough state this is most useful, but if most of the wood arrives machine planed it is better to sharpen the plane as at figure 69 (e) and use it like a small trying plane.

The sharpening of plane irons is never an easy task for the beginner but the job can be simplified by using a honing guide (fig 69g). This device locks onto the blade and helps achieve a constant sharpening angle.

MAINTENANCE OF HAND TOOLS

Much of the advice already given applies equally well to the special planes. Take care to assemble the block and shoulder planes with the blade bevel upwards. Sharpening the golf club shape cutters of the router is not easy. They should be sharpened on the bevelled side only, merely wiping off the wire edge on the flat side. Place the oilstone on the edge of the bench so that the stem of the cutter can hang down. Occasional regrinding will be necessary and this can be done on the side of the grinding wheel.

☐ SAWS

If treated properly a good quality saw will last a lifetime. It requires sharpening at least once a year, but it is probably the one tool that most amateurs neglect to sharpen, probably because they fail to understand how the saw works. Much has been written concerning this point in Chapter 2, but a few additional points may be helpful here.

The bluntness of the teeth may not be readily apparent, but each time the saw is used the teeth become a little more worn, losing their keen edge (fig 70a). This will be recognised as a dull glint of light on the points of the teeth, the light being reflected by the dulled edges. Any truly sharp edge, be it a chisel, plane blade or saw tooth, cannot be seen. A saw with dulled teeth will require needless effort and eventually the blade will jamb in the cut as the teeth lose their set.

Misuse of a saw will result in broken teeth, or if the saw has been badly sharpened in the past then the teeth may be uneven (fig 70b). A saw consists of a gang of teeth and each tooth must do its fair share of the work. The first stage in sharpening the teeth of a saw must therefore be to level them out with a long flat file. Even a saw in good condition should have the teeth 'topped' in this way before sharpening. The blade can be held in a special saw vice which grips the saw near the roots of the teeth (fig 70k). It is usually advantageous to remove the saw handle from the blade before the latter is clamped in the vice. Top the teeth of the saw by running the file lengthwise down them. Discontinue filing when the smallest of the teeth have been touched (fig 70c).

If the teeth have been badly mishapen by previous efforts at sharpening, then they will need reshaping with a triangular

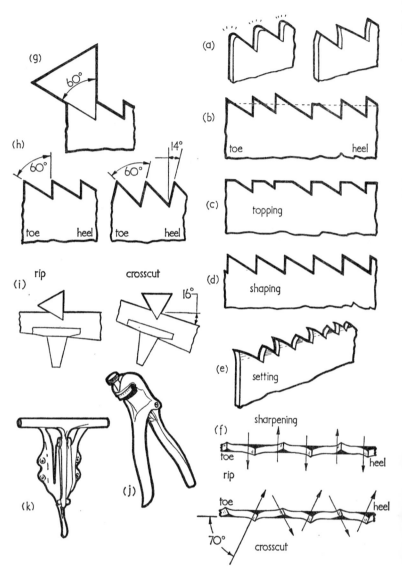

Fig 70 Sharpening saws: (*a*) dulled teeth, (*b*) irregular and broken teeth, (*c*) topping with a flat file, (*d*) shaping with a triangular file, (*e*) spring setting, (*f*) sharpening rip and crosscut, (*g*) choice of file size, (*h*) shape of rip and crosscut teeth, (*i*) sloping the saw when sharpening crosscut saw, (*j*) plier type saw set and (*k*) saw sharpening vice

file. Choose a file sufficiently large that, having been used once and turned to present a new face to the work, part of the old blunt surface is not in contact with a tooth (fig 70g). The file manufacturers recommend that a worn file be used to sharpen the teeth of a new saw. Treat the file with respect as a slip may not only damage the saw, but it may also damage the teeth of the file. Keep the file clean with a wire brush. A new file can be rubbed with chalk to prevent metal clogging (pinning) the teeth. Never stack the files against each other, and store them in a dry place to prevent rust.

It must be remembered that the teeth of the rip saw have to be shaped differently from the teeth of the crosscut saw. Figure 70 (h) shows that the gullet angle of all hand saw teeth is 60°. This is the reason for using a triangular file. However, the leading edge of the tooth of a rip saw is vertical, whereas the leading edge of the tooth of a crosscut saw leans back through an angle of 14°. The correct shape tooth for the rip saw is achieved relatively easily, but the crosscut saw is most difficult. It is useful therefore to be able to slope the saw and saw vice through 16° when sharpening the crosscut saw. This puts the back of the file in the horizontal plane (fig 70i). File the teeth straight across at this stage until they are all even and the small flat on the top of each tooth has just been removed.

The third stage of the work is setting the teeth. Hand saws are spring set. That is to say the teeth are bent outwards alternately (fig 70e). The best setting is generally considered to be done with a hammer, and indeed some modern saw factories set their best quality saws in this fashion. The saw is placed on a chamfered metal block and every other tooth tapped over. The saw blade is then turned over so that the other teeth may be bent to a similar extent. In this process only the top half of the tooth is bent; otherwise cracking is liable to occur at the base of each tooth. The alternative method of setting a saw is by using the plier type saw set (fig 70j). This is a self-contained tool that is adjustable to suit handsaws from 4 to 12 points. It is built like a pair of pliers. When the handles are squeezed together, the tool first grips the saw and then sets the top half of each tooth to the required angle.

The fourth stage of the work is the sharpening of the saw. This is performed with the file that was used for sharpening the teeth. The file is always held in the horizontal plane. With the rip saw it is taken straight across; with the crosscut saw the file is held at an angle of 70° to the blade (fig 70f).

Often all that is required is a light topping, followed by sharpening. The tenon saw can be sharpened as a crosscut saw, but the dovetail saw with tiny teeth is more easily sharpened straight across. Occasionally the backed saws will require re-tensioning. This can be done with gentle blows of the hammer as explained in Chapter 2.

☐ CABINET SCRAPER AND PLANE

The cutting action of the cabinet scraper depends on the quality of the burr put on the edge of the blade. The edge must be trued with a long second cut file (fig 71). Hold the blade in the vice and, keeping the file lengthwise on, file a few strokes making the edge flat and square. This edge may be further trued on an oilstone. Rub both the edge and sides of the blade in turn to produce an accurate 90° corner. This corner has to be bent outwards to form the burr. Replace the blade in the vice and, using either a special tool of hardened steel called a burnisher or the back of a gouge, pass this firmly down the edge at 90° to the surface of the blade. Tilt the burnisher through 10° and make another pass pressing firmly to polish the edge. One more pass at 15° to the horizontal will cause sufficient burr to be pushed out for the scraper to cut cleanly.

Instructions for sharpening the scraper plane are usually supplied with the tool. The cutter is ground at 45° but it must

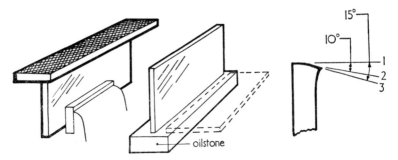

Fig 71 Sharpening the cabinet scraper: file the edge flat then oilstone the surfaces and burnish the edge over to create a burr

be sharpened before it can be used by polishing the ground surface with a fine or medium oilstone. This should throw up a burr on the flat side but this burr must be removed by rubbing the blade flat on the oilstone. A much stronger burr can be created by using a burnisher. Burnish first the flat side, holding the burnisher flat to the surface of the blade. This will consolidate the metal. Then place the blade in the vice and start burnishing on the 45° bevel. Work steadily and press quite hard, raising the burnisher through 30° until it is 15° below the horizontal (fig 72).

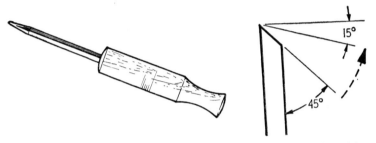

Fig 72   Sharpening the scraper plane: *(left)* hardened steel burnisher; *(right)* burnishing the blade

☐   SCREWDRIVER

Several screwdrivers should be bought and ground or filed to fit screws of differing sizes. The blade should be the same width as the bottom of the slot in the screw head (fig 73). This will prevent the screwdriver from scoring the work. The blade should be just sufficiently thin to fit to the bottom of the slot. When filing or grinding a screwdriver do so across the blade; it will hold the screw more securely. Always keep the thickness of the blade even at the tip. Do not file to an extreme taper shape or it will cause the screwdriver to jump from the slot when pressure is applied.

☐   SPOKESHAVE

The blade of the spokeshave is sharpened like the cutter of a smoothing plane. The problem is that of size. A block of wood with a saw cut at one end (fig 74) can act as a useful holder, helping one maintain a firm grip when sharpening the blade on the oilstone. The blade of the wooden spokeshave

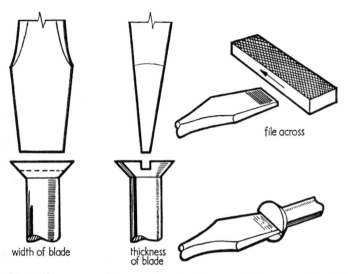

width of blade   thickness of blade   file across

Fig 73   Filing a screwdriver to size. By filing carefully across the blade, the screwdriver can be made to grip the screw firmly

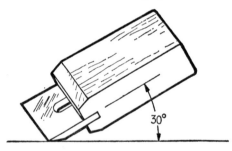

30°

Fig 74   Shapening the blade of a spokeshave. This is sharpened as a plane iron or chisel. A wooden holder helps one to grip the blade

is another problem. The usual method is to hold the blade steady in the vice and move the oilstone over the cutting edge.

☐ TWIST DRILLS

Twist drills for use in the hand or electric drill are sharpened on the high-speed grinding wheel. This difficult technique can only be mastered with practice. Figure 75 should help to explain it. Choose a fairly large drill as the smaller sizes make it difficult to see what is happening.

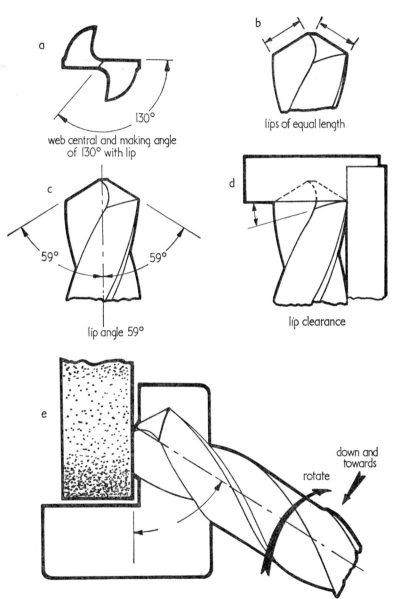

a

130°

web central and making angle
of 130° with lip

b

lips of equal length

c

59°   59°

lip angle 59°

d

lip clearance

e

down and
towards

rotate

Fig 75 Sharpening a twist drill. This is performed on the
high speed grinding wheel

The drill is applied to the side of the wheel and has to be rotated about its axis in order to create a new surface on the end. This will produce a sharp cutting edge. If one just rotates the drill in this fashion then the end of the drill will be cone-shaped. Any cutting edge must have clearance to cut. A cone-shaped drill would simply rub on the work. Start with the cutting edge against the wheel; as the drill is rotated clockwise so the tip of the drill is brought up on the wheel by dropping the hands downward and towards the body (fig 75e). This will back off the cutting edge and give the clearance required. The same movement is repeated with the other cutting edge on the drill.

Checks can be applied to see that the drill is correctly sharpened. The point, or chisel, should be central and should make an angle of 130° with the cutting edge, or lip (fig 75a). The lips should be of equal length (fig 75b). The lips should be at an angle of 59° to the axis of the drill (fig 75c), and when checked with a try square there should be a little lip clearance

□ VICE

The vice is the most important part of the equipment. Get inside the bench from time to time and oil the screw thread. Check the jaws of the vice and renew the packing if necessary. Sometimes the jaws become so polished with use that they require roughening to give a better grip to the work. This can be done with a rasp or Surform.

Chapter 5

Timber

GROWTH OF A TREE

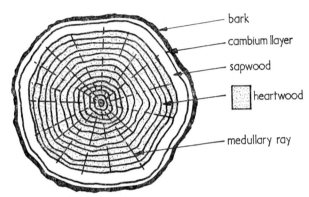

Fig 76 Cross-section through a tree to show names of principal parts

A cross-section of a tree (fig 76) reveals many features result-ing from its growth. The new wood cells form a band just under the bark which is always present but not clearly dis-tinguishable in every species. The band, usually paler in colour than the rest of the tree, is called the sapwood.

The sapwood of a tree is of little use, being soft and prone to attack by fungi and beetles. The useful part of the tree, the heartwood, is composed of older cells that are no longer grow-ing.

Probably the most noticeable features on the end of a log are the concentric circles called annual rings. Each ring gener-ally indicates one year's growth, so by counting the rings from the bark to the centre of the tree one can calculate the tree's age. The annual rings are formed by the difference between the spring growth and the summer growth. Spring growth, being the most rapid, is the lighter, greater part of each ring. It is usually softer and more porous than the thinner and darker band of summer growth.

At right angles to the annual rings are the medullary rays.

G

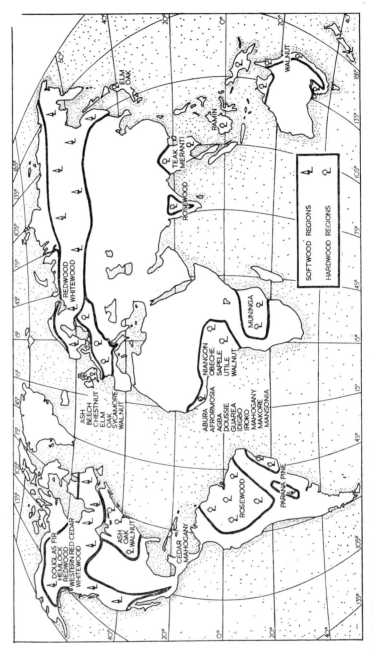

Fig 77 A general guide showing the chief sources of hardwoods and softwoods

These are more discernible in some woods than others. In oak, for instance, they are particularly attractive.

HARDWOOD AND SOFTWOOD

Commercially, timber can be divided into two groups, hardwood and softwood. This description is, however, misleading. For instance a hardwood like balsa can be softer than some softwoods, while a softwood such as yew can be quite hard.

Softwood is the generic term for timber produced from coniferous trees. With certain unimportant exceptions these are the evergreens and are easily distinguishable by scale or needle type leaves. There are two types of softwood. The first, commonly known as European redwood, but also called Scots pine, or red or yellow deal, is the most important structural and general purpose timber in Europe. Most of the timber in our houses, the rafters, flooring, and second fittings, is European redwood. The second type of softwood is called European whitewood, or Norway or European spruce. It is familiar to everyone as the Christmas tree. Besides having the same uses as redwood, whitewood is also the principal raw material for the manufacture of wood pulp for newsprint.

Hardwood is the generic term for deciduous trees. These timbers are used for fine cabinet making. Such timbers are grown in warmer climates than the softwood trees. The variety of hardwood timbers compared with softwoods is enormous, but despite the wide range the trade in softwoods is nine times larger than the trade in hardwoods. Softwood is both strong and cheap and has extensive uses from window frames in the building industry to packing cases for exports.

CONVERSION

The conversion of timber means cutting the log into useful thicknesses of board to obtain the greatest quantity of good quality timber possible.

Plain or through and through sawing is the quickest and least expensive method of conversion as there is little wastage

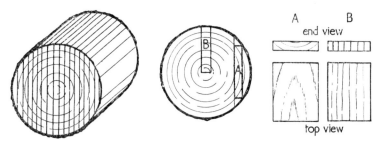

Fig 78 Slash sawing, also known as plain or through and
through conversion

(fig 78). This is therefore the most common method of con-
verting a log into planks. Many of the boards cut this way are
tangentially sawn. That is to say they are cut tangential to the
annual rings. Some of the middle boards however are cut at
right angles to the annual rings, and these are said to be
radially or quarter sawn (fig 78).

Some woods possess particularly attractive features and are
sawn in a deliberate fashion to reveal their most decorative
surface, sometimes called the silver grain or figure of the wood.
It is revealed by cutting planks along the line of the medullary rays (quarter sawing).

The method of quarter sawing shown in figure 79 (left) is
expensive and leads to a great amount of wastage. It is therefore more usual for a log to be quarter sawn as shown in figure
79 (right). Although such timber is not truly quarter sawn
this method will produce many decorative boards. As well as
producing a good figure, quarter sawn timber is very stable.

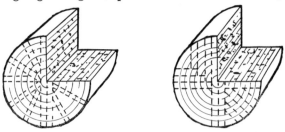

Fig 79 Quarter sawn oak: *(left)* is the only method of conversion that
will produce solely quarter sawn boards; *(right)* shows economical
methods of quarter sawing. This shows two less wasteful methods of
obtaining boards that are all nearly quarter sawn

This factor can at times be more important than the figure on the surface of the timber.

To reveal the full flame figure in a softwood such as Douglas fir (Columbian pine) the log must be tangentially sawn. However, boards cut in this manner have the disadvantage of cupping. They do not keep their shape as well as quarter sawn boards.

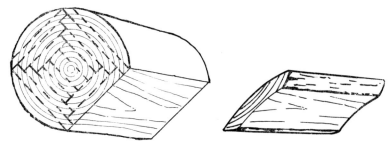

Figs 80 & 81 Method of tangentially sawing a log, and disadvantage of tangential sawing. This produces a flame figure that is most attractive in Douglas Fir. Unfortunately tangentially sawn boards are liable to cup

SEASONING

The timber is seasoned (dried) at a controlled rate to remove the sap. Seasoned timber has many advantages, the chief one being that it is less likely to shrink or warp. It is also easier to work on, and will polish, paint, or varnish better. Because such timber is also lighter in weight it is easier to handle. It is also less likely to be attacked by fungi.

☐ AIR OR NATURAL SEASONING

In this traditional method of seasoning the planks of wood are stacked neatly, leaving a space between each plank with a sticker to allow the air to circulate and carry away the excess moisture. The weight of the stack also keeps the planks flat. When one has to store timber for a period of time this is the way it should be done. The stickers must be placed accurately in line one above the other to prevent distortion of the lower boards. The planks at the bottom are built up off the ground away from frost and dew.

A good roof will shed the rain and prevent the heat of the sun drying the timber too rapidly. Fast drying of the timber can cause surface cracks to appear. It is usual for boards in the seasoning process to be end coated to prevent rapid drying from the ends. The coating can be thick paint or paraffin wax applied hot.

The type of seasoning shed described will ensure that the timber is open to the wind but not the sun or rain. Under such conditions an inch (25mm) thick plank takes one year to season. Every additional inch (25mm) increase in thickness of board requires another year of seasoning.

☐   KILN OR ARTIFICIAL SEASONING

A quicker method of seasoning is kiln or artificial seasoning. This is an industrial process and requires a kiln in which warm air and steam can be circulated by means of fans. The rate of drying and the final moisture content of the timber in the kiln is controlled by adjusting the temperature and humidity of the circulating air.

Depending upon the timber, kiln seasoning can take from three days to three weeks. It is a skilled job the success of which is reflected in the way the timber can be utilised after seasoning. Bad drying can result in loose knots, twisted timber, and fuzzy grain that is awkward to plane.

MOISTURE CONTENT

Wood will absorb or give up moisture until the moisture content of the wood is in equilibrium with the surrounding air. It is possible by kiln seasoning to extract all the moisture from the wood. This, however, is seldom required as bone dry timber will only take on moisture to suit the conditions in the workshop, and will later change that moisture content to suit the conditions existing in its final surroundings. This happens despite the thicknesses of polish, paint or hard varnish. Everyone knows that on a wet day wooden windows and doors can stick, whereas on a hot summer day they may rattle in their frames. The expansion and contraction of timber is due to the taking on or giving up of moisture.

It is important to the timber merchant, particularly when kiln seasoning, that the moisture content of the timber in stock is accurately assessed from a fair sample. This is done by excluding the wood from the first 9in (230mm) of a plank. The sample piece is first weighed, then dried in an oven until bone dry. As it cannot be seen at a glance when the sample is bone dry, it is usual to weigh when it is thought to be dry, then place back in the oven for a further twenty minutes before reweighing. If the second reading is the same as the first then it is safe to assume that the figure represents the oven dry weight. The moisture content of the sample can then be calculated as follows:

$$\frac{\text{weight of wet timber—weight of oven dry timber}}{\text{weight of oven dry timber}} \times 100 = \begin{array}{l}\text{moisture}\\\text{content}\end{array}$$

$$\text{ie,} \quad \frac{\text{wt of moisture}}{\text{wt of oven dry timber}} \times 100 = \text{moisture content}$$

It is possible with very wet stock to have moisture content readings of well over 100% as there can be a greater weight of moisture in the sample than the timber. Air seasoned timber will generally reach a level of about 20%. Further drying necessitates the use of a kiln. It is usual for the craftsman to bring the wood indoors for a short period before it is used; this can reduce the moisture content to about 14% which is suitable for most applications. Placing the stock in a situation with a high degree of central heating can however reduce the moisture content even further to about 10%.

TIMBER DEFECTS

A defect in timber is any flaw that can affect the strength or the appearance of the finished article. Figure 82 shows the major faults found in unselected stock. The most common defects are known as shakes (splits); the name of the shake often refers to the pattern these splits have formed.

A heartshake is caused by decay at the centre of the tree

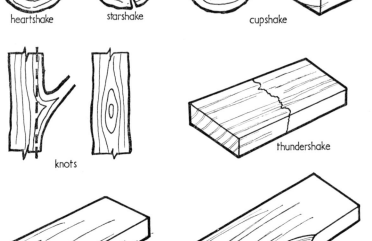

heartshake   starshake   cupshake

knots

thundershake

end checks   waney edge

Fig 82 Timber defects. Any of these can spoil the work. Look out for
them when selecting timber

spreading along the lines of the medullary rays. It can largely
be prevented if the tree is not allowed to lie too long in log
form.

A star shake is caused by the drying and shrinkage of the
log more rapidly on the outside than at the heart. The splits
occur along the line of the medullary rays.

Cup shakes occur between the annual rings in the spring
wood, due to the inner part of the wood shrinking from the
outer layer. This often happens with pine and fir trees but is
usually small and not a serious defect.

Knots are the cross sections of branches. Live knots are firm
in place whereas dead knots are loose or have fallen out.
Knots weaken the timber but can be placed to look attractive.

A thunder shake is a crack across the grain which is probably caused by bad felling. African mahoganies are prone to this defect.

Checks are small splits, usually not more than 2-4in (50-100mm) long, which occur at the ends of long lengths of wood which have dried too rapidly during seasoning. This can largely be prevented by end coating as noted earlier.

Wane is the natural edge of the tree that remains on the plank after conversion. It may have the bark left on. It is best to work well inside the waney edge of a board in order to avoid the sapwood, the latter, as has been mentioned, being prone to attack by insects.

SHRINKAGE

As the timber dries out the loss of water will result in shrinkage and warping. Figure 83 shows the end view of a log with various boards indicated. Tangential shrinkage is nearly twice that of radial shrinkage. The tangentially sawn board will also tend to cup, as though the annual rings try to straighten when they shrink. The board cups away from the heart side. To overcome this stack the timber carefully during the seasoning process. The weight of the stack will hold such boards flat between the stickers. When glueing several boards together, it is usual to arrange the pattern of the end grain as shown in figure 83 to keep warping to a minimum. Occasionally a wide board will warp but this can be partially corrected by damping the cupped (hollow) side of the board to swell the pores. The board is then left over-night with weights on top to hold it flat.

The quarter sawn plank shown in figure 83 is very stable. The round stock, however, will shrink to an oval section and square stock cut in the fashion indicated tends to a diamond shape. Because of diamonding the stocks of the best wooden jack planes are selected so that the annual rings cross them from side to side. Such wood will not distort from the square section.

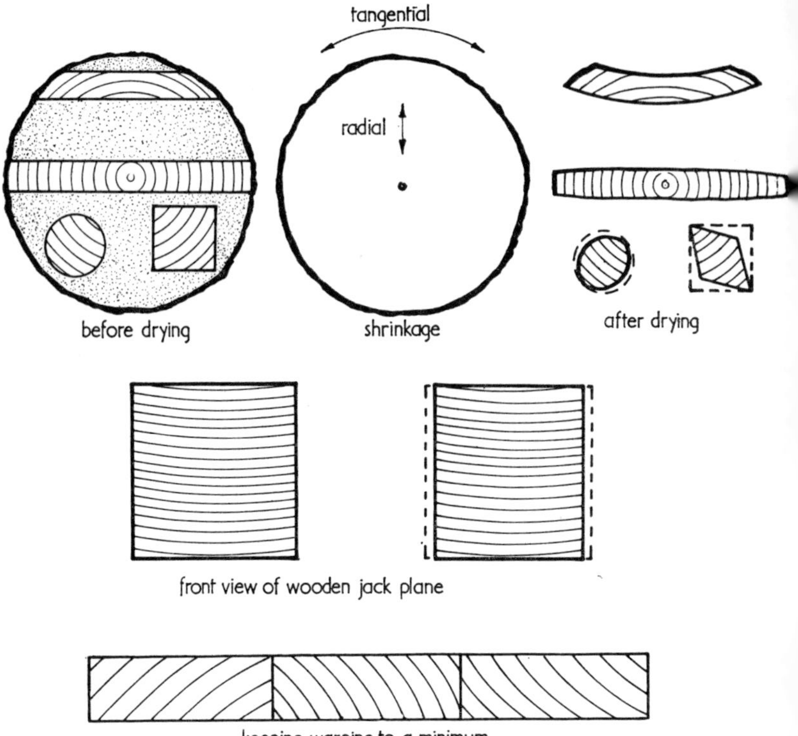

Fig 83 Shrinkage and change of shape during seasoning. Select timber carefully as it can change shape even after drying. Quarter sawn boards are always the best, but are not freely available. Stack wide boards between stickers prior to use and this will keep them flat. Note the care taken in the selection of wood for the stock of a wooden plane. When edge jointing boards, avoid placing the grain the same way in each piece

STORAGE OF TIMBER

The quality of timber can be easily reduced by bad storage. It can decay, warp, and split if handled incorrectly. Timber bought as seasoned stock is unlikely to be sufficiently dry to withstand the rigours of a centrally heated house or workshop. Such stock should be stored in a cool dry place. If the material feels dry then it may be worked on immediately. Otherwise it should be stored for a period of time.

The only acceptable alternative to stacking timber is to stand the boards upright. This will prevent bowing of the planks along their length but cannot prevent cupping. On no account should one leave the timber in an untidy heap, or leave a plank leaning against a wall as the wood will take on a permanent sag.

SOME TIMBERS AVAILABLE

The following is a list of some of the woods suitable for use by the home craftsman. When selecting boards from the timber yard do not be put off by the grimy surface of some of the stock. This surface dirt is in no way a defect but rather an indication that the stock is well seasoned. The grimy exterior will soon be removed by one or two shavings of the plane.

☐ HARDWOODS

Abura (West Africa) A pale, reddish to light-brown wood with an even texture. Very stable when seasoned. Resistant to acids. Works well and cleanly by hand and machine. It takes a good finish but it lacks character in its appearance.

Afrormosia (West Africa) A brownish-yellow timber with darker streaks often thought of as a substitute for teak. It is, however, a fine wood in its own right, and a good show-wood. It is extremely durable and has good resistance to decay. It is the worst timber for the problem of colour change, no finish being available to prevent this.

Agba (West Africa) Light yellow in colour, straight grained with a fairly close, even texture. It has good durability and is very resistant to decay. It works well and is largely used as an alternative to oak.

Ash (Europe and America) Pale yellow in colour and usually straight grained. This is a tough and flexible timber and is used chiefly for sports goods and tool handles. It has good bending properties and is invaluable for bent wood furniture.

Beech (Europe) Pinkish-red to yellow-brown in colour and usually straight grained with a fine texture. It is exceptionally strong, and machines and works well. It is a good wood for chairs, tool handles, planes, benches, and is widely used in the furniture industry. It holds tacks well, and is therefore used for the frames of upholstered furniture.

Cedar (British Honduras) Pinkish-brown in colour, it resembles true mahogany, but is lighter in weight. It is easily recognised by its characteristic scent which is so familiar because of its use in cigar boxes. It is fully resistant to decay and therefore used in boatbuilding, but is also used for the linings of wardrobes and chests, and for the bottoms of drawers on account of its moth-resistant qualities and pleasing aroma.

Chestnut, Sweet (Europe) Yellow-brown in colour and sometimes used as a substitute for oak. It works and finishes well but is rather soft.

Doussie, Afzelia (West Africa) Strong, durable and light brown in colour. It is a high grade wood producing a good finish and has a wide variety of uses similar to Iroko and Teak. It has a low shrinkage factor.

Elm (Great Britain, Holland, Japan) A light brown wood with distinctive grain pattern. It is strong and durable and does not cleave easily. It is resistant to decay under water. It is used for furniture, wheelmaking, coffins, and boat building. Generally a rather handsome timber. Japanese Elm is milder and more straight grained than English Elm.

Guarea (West Africa) Pinkish brown in colour, with a fine texture and cedar-like scent. It is fairly mild and easy to work. It is probably closer in appearance and properties to Cuban and American (Honduras) mahogany than any other timber. Its lack of dimensional movement makes it popular for drawer sides. It has good finishing properties. Its chief disadvantage is that dust from this timber is very irritating.

Idigbo (West Africa) A large tree providing timber that is pale yellow to light brown in colour with little distinction between heartwood and sapwood. Resistant to decay. It is soft to medium hard and can be easily worked by hand or machine. Not a widely known timber.

Iroko (West Africa) This wood is yellow in colour when freshly cut, but on exposure to light quickly becomes a rich golden brown. It is well figured and extremely handsome. Its strength compares with that of home-grown oak and it is very resistant to fungus and insect attack. Owing to its resistance to wear and to acids and its durability under damp conditions, it is particularly suitable for bench tops and workshops.

Mahogany (West Africa) This timber is mid-red in colour and is probably the most widely used of the mahoganies at present. Many of the logs are 6ft (up to 2m) across and can produce very wide boards. It is coarser in texture than Honduras mahogany and sometimes has an interlocked grain which produces an attractive figure but is difficult to plane by hand. It has small dimensional movement and is often used for drawer sides.

Mahogany, Honduras (British Honduras) This is one of the finest woods, being stable and extremely strong. It works well with all types of tools, and glues and finishes well. It is durable and has many uses, but is rather expensive.

Makore (West Africa) This wood is similar to a close grained mahogany but with a much finer texture. Makore is also denser, harder and heavier than mahogany. It is often used for high-class work.

Mansonia (West Africa) The heartwood is a purple-brown. It is a fairly hard timber, usually with a straight grain, and has a smooth and fine texture. It is a durable timber and makes a substitute for walnut. It is used for much high-class work. Its chief disadvantage is that dust from this wood can be particularly irritating.

Meranti, Light Red (SE Asia) As its name suggests this wood is red in colour. It works well and is suitable for general interior work. Pinhole-borer attack can cause wastage if the timber is not carefully selected.

Muninga (East Africa) This timber has a warm brown colour and a pleasing grain pattern. It is mild, stable, and works well by hand and machine. It has good finishing properties and is an excellent show-wood. Its only disadvantage, compared to species such as teak and afrormosia, is that logs sometimes contain some white spotting which can look unsightly, but this can to a great extent be overcome in the finishing process.

Niangon (West Africa) This is a reddish wood similar to African mahogany in all respects except that it has a rather more open grain and, when quarter sawn, shows dark flecks on the rays. It is quite popular in the furniture trade.

Oak (European) A creamy yellow wood with a distinctive grain. If cut on the quarter the medullary rays are revealed as an attractive feature. This wood is immensely strong and durable; however it splits easily and the grain is open. This wood is at present out of fashion in modern domestic furniture but this should not deter the hand craftsman.

Oak, American (N America) American oaks are divided into two classes, white oak and red oak. White oak approximates to European oak, with a pinkish tinge. Red oak, as its name implies, is pinky-red in colour, harder and coarser, and not durable. The white oak can be used instead of European oak.

Oak, Japanese (Japan) This oak is different in character from oaks native to Europe and the Americas. It is mild and more easily worked, lighter in weight, and reliable. It is not suitable for exterior work but can be used for all classes of furniture. The appearance of the European species is, however, often preferred.

Oak, Slavonian (Yugoslavia) European oaks vary considerably according to conditions of growth. Slavonian oak, which grows in very suitable conditions, is of slow even growth, of uniform colour and straight grain. It is mild and easy to work and has a handsome figure when quarter sawn. It is used for church work and wherever the highest class work in oak is required.

Obeche (West Africa) This timber is creamy-white to pale yellow in colour and light in weight. It is fairly soft, but firm and fine in texture. Obeche is one of the largest of the forest trees of West Africa and from its cylindrical trunk, clean timber of exceptional lengths is obtainable. This timber is popular because of its reliability in quality and dimensional stability.

It is used mainly in the field of lower-priced domestic cabinet work and in kitchen furniture.

Ramin (Sarawak) This timber is of uniform pale straw colour, moderately hard and heavy. It is very clean and straight grained and for this reason used extensively for picture frames and small mouldings. Ramin is valued for its strength and similarity to beech as a general utility wood. It paints, varnishes and machines well. It is generally unsuitable for use in large sections because of its tendency to checking.

Rosewood, Rio (Brazil) A rich reddish-brown wood with contrasting dark grain markings. A very decorative wood suitable for high-glass interior work and makes most impressive furniture. Its chief disadvantage is that a purple dust from the wood will stain the hands and clothes.

Rosewood, Bombay (India) This wood is slightly plainer in appearance than the Brazilian timber. It is suitable for high-class cabinet work but requires careful polishing.

Sapele (West Africa) Of typical mahogany colour, Sapele is characterised by a marked and regular stripe, particularly prominent on quarter sawn surfaces. Harder and heavier than African mahogany it is, nevertheless, very similar in appearance. It is a tough, hard timber, resistant to decay. It works well by hand and machine tools, but can be difficult to hand plane due to its interlocking grain.

Sycamore (Europe) Milky white weathering to a golden yellow colour, this is an easy timber to work. Being tasteless it is often used when wood has to come in contact with food. It is used in furniture mainly as a contrast to other woods, in the form of decorative inlay or beading. It is sometimes used for the sides and bottoms of drawers.

Teak (Burma) This timber varies in grain and colour from a clear golden shade to a chocolate brown. It is one of the most valuable and expensive of all woods, being extremely durable, strong, stable, resistant to moisture, termites, fire, acids and non-corrosive. It has a wide range of uses including furniture, garden furniture, laboratory bench tops, and ships' decking. Afrormosia is a good substitute for teak since it is not so expensive. However, as teak presents less of a problem with colour-change, this can be a false economy. It is a popular timber for furniture, being a good show-wood.

Utile (West Africa) Utile is a mahogany coloured wood, very even in colour and texture. Although similar to Sapele, it is more stable and is one of the most popular hardwoods. It is very resistant to decay and works well. It has been found a very satisfactory timber for drawer sides.

Walnut, African (West Africa) This is not a true walnut, but a very handsome wood, golden brown in colour with occasional thin black streaks and a lustrous surface. It is sometimes re-ferred to as Nigerian Golden Walnut and often used for high-class work.

Walnut, American Black (USA) This is a handsome wood of a rich dark brown colour, which works easily and takes a fine finish. It is of medium-heavy weight. It is a true walnut, re-lated to the European species, and used in high-quality work.

Walnut (European) This wood has an unusually wide range of colour that may vary from a cold grey to a warm brown. The grain can vary from a straight pattern to a flowery con-trast. It is the favourite of all woods, being excellent to work and taking a good finish. It is used only for high-quality work, but increasing difficulty is found in obtaining good quality solid timber, especially of English walnut. French and Italian walnut are fairly satisfactory substitutes.

Walnut, Australian (Queensland, Australia) This is neither a true walnut nor is it related to African walnut. The quarter sawn boards can show an attractive figure.

☐ SOFTWOODS
Douglas Fir, Columbian Pine (British Columbia, and some British) The heartwood is reddish to brownish in background colour, with a darker, very prominent growth ring figure, often quite attractive in appearance. The grain is usually straight but may be slightly wavy, while the texture is moder-ately coarse. The yellow background is soft whereas the darker growth rings are quite hard. This timber has excellent

strength qualities, is very knot-free, and is used extensively for ladder construction. It is highly water resistant.

Hemlock, Western (Canada and NW USA) This wood is pale yellowish-brown in colour, sometimes with a faint red tinge. It is straight-grained and has a moderately fine texture. This is a general utility wood often classed as a whitewood.

Parana Pine (South America) This timber is variable in colour from light to dark brown, and often marked with distinctive bright red streaks. The grain is normally straight and the texture moderately fine and even. It takes varnish and paint well, and is usually available in knot-free lengths.

Redwood, Scots Pine, Red Deal, Yellow Deal (Russia, Baltic countries, Scandinavia, Canada, and some British) The colour is light reddish-brown or yellowish-brown. It is moderately resinous but usually straight grained. It has fairly good strength properties and works, nails and finishes well. Red-wood is more frequently used where painting over is not necessary, being usually left bare on the interior of built-in cupboards, or given a clear finish.

Whitewood, European Spruce ie Christmas Tree (Russia, Baltic countries, Scandinavia, Canada, and some British) This is very light yellowish-brown in colour, almost white. It has a mildly lustrous surface when planed and is very slightly resin-ous. The grain is straight and the texture moderately even. Its use is usually confined to cupboard framing.

Yew (Europe) The heartwood is reddish when freshly cut, but soon darkens to a deep orange-brown that often shows an attractive growth ring figure. It is finely and uniformly tex-tured, and straight grained. For a softwood species it is very heavy. It was used in the early days for archers' bows. The leaves of this tree are poisonous to animals and so its growth is generally confined to churchyards, and it is not in plentiful supply. It is occasionally used for high-class furniture.

H

VENEER

A veneer is a thin slice of wood usually taken from a species showing attractive grain or figure. It can be an economical way of making an attractive item of furniture, as a veneer of expensive show-wood can be used to cover a groundwork of cheaper timber. Using veneers can also conserve rare and exotic woods, making a little go a long way. In some instances there may be insufficient timber available in a certain colour, grain pattern, or figure to be able to make an item of reasonable size from the solid wood. Modern adhesives help to form veneers into new and exciting shapes. Sometimes a fundamental part of the design is impossible to construct in the solid wood. Techniques of lamination and veneering on particle board have produced new fashions in furniture design. However, those master craftsmen as far back as Chippendale, Sheraton and Hepplewhite used mahogany veneers in their work, as did the Egyptians 3,000 years ago.

Veneers are cut from the bole of the tree, above the roots up to the first limb. Veneer can be made using a saw or a knife. Saw cutting is very wasteful and is now reserved for extremely hard woods, difficult woods such as curls, small diameter logs, and when a thick veneer is required.

Prior to knife cutting a veneer, the log has to be softened by steaming in a vat, from a few hours to several weeks according to the hardness of the wood and the thickness of the cut to be taken. Machinery is employed that moves either the knife or the log. Veneer is cut from the log to a determined thickness which can be as thin as a few thousandths of an inch and as thick as 5/16in (0.1mm-8mm).

There are two traditional methods of laying veneer, the hammer and caul methods. The hammer method involves the use of a veneering hammer. This tool is a handled wooden block, one edge of which is fitted with a strip of brass. The hammer is used to press on the veneer and push out surplus glue from underneath the veneer.

Prior to laying veneer the groundwork should be keyed to permit maximum adhesion. This is done with a toothing plane, a wooden plane with a serrated edge cutter set at a high pitch angle.

Brush a thin even coat of scotch glue (see chapter 6) on the groundwork and allow to tack. Lay the veneer in position and press down. Lightly sponge the veneer with hot water then work an electric iron over it with the control at silk. The iron should be hot but not hot enough to cause water to spit on the sole. The heat from the iron will melt the glue and draw it up into the pores of the veneer. An iron that is too hot will allow the glue to penetrate the surface of the veneer and this will cause discolouration. With the veneer hammer work squeegee fashion to exclude air from under the veneer and to force out surplus glue. The sequence of damping, ironing and working with the veneer hammer can be repeated many times until the job is finished.

Simple joins can be made with the grain of the veneer by laying the first veneer, overlapping the second by an inch (25mm), then cutting through both veneers using a sharp knife and straight edge. Remove the surplus from the top veneer then lift the veneer slightly to peel away the strip from underneath. Iron the veneer back home and place gummed tape across the join to prevent a gap forming by contraction of the veneer. Always trim the veneers to size after the glue has set.

The method of caul veneering is suggested for the veneered box (chapter 9). It is simpler since it requires less equipment. Again the veneer is cut oversize. The groundwork is prepared flat and true and a caul is made from $\frac{3}{4}$in (19mm) blockboard or similar. The caul should be just larger than the work in hand.

A synthetic resin glue should be used. Spread the glue evenly on the groundwork taking special care to glue the edges. Place the veneer in position and a clean sheet of paper (not newsprint) on top of the veneer in case glue should penetrate to the surface. The caul is then placed on top and pressure is applied with G cramps. On large work thick crossbearers are used to spread the pressure of the cramps.

Most of the timbers listed in the section dealing with hardwoods are available as veneers. Certain more important additions are as follows.

Olive Ash (UK) Attractive contrasting light and olive colour

Figured African Cherry (W Africa) An exceptionally highly figured block mottle veneer. The plain veneer is referred to as makore.

Eucalyptus (Australian) Rather an unusual colour, pink to beige, and can be beautifully mottled. It is available in long lengths.

Lacewood (UK) A pink, highly figured veneer with attractive lace rays.

Figured Indian Laurel (India) Dark rich colour and attractively figured. It can be used successfully in association with other lighter timbers.

Bird's Eye Maple (N America) A cream colour veneer which has unique figure, with masses of tiny eyes or knot formations.

West Indian Satinwood (W India and Ceylon) A golden colour, stripy, with beeswing mottled figure. Once very much used for cabinet work. When well figured it has a depth of light not seen in other woods. It takes and holds a polish well. The colour remains fast.

Tola (W Africa) A reddish, straight grained, striped veneer widely used by veneered chipboard manufacturers.

Figured Willow (UK) A creamy golden colour. This veneer is exceptionally attractive and usually well figured.

Zebrano (Africa) As the name implies, a contrasting light and dark stripy wood. It is straw colour with brown stripes, generally used in small decorative pieces.

MANUFACTURED BOARDS

☐ PLYWOOD

Plywood is made from three or more odd number of wood veneers glued face to face with a suitable adhesive and with the grain of each veneer running at right-angles to its neighbour. Plywood is many times stronger in bending strength than its equivalent thickness of solid wood, and is available in very large panels. By varying the species, thickness of veneer

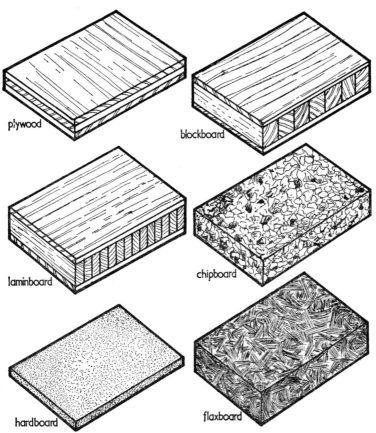

Fig 84 Manufactured boards. All these boards are available in very
large sheets. Their rate of expansion and contraction in changing
humidity is negligible, and apart from plywood, they will not warp

and type of glue it is possible to manufacture plywood for a
great variety of purposes. One instance of this is the waterproof plywood used for building marine craft which will
withstand exposure to weather, immersion in water, and is
unaffected by micro organisms.

Plywood is commonly used when making furniture but it
is generally restricted to the cheaper and more every day items
such as the backing of framed kitchen cuboards and cabinets,
and shelves and drawer-bottoms. The disadvantages of ply-

wood are that it can warp, and that it has an ugly edge. Remember that plywood is always stronger in one direction than the other. Advantage can usually be made of this when designing an item.

☐ BLOCKBOARD AND LAMINBOARD

These board materials are made from long narrow strips of wood, edge-glued together and veneered both sides. Blockboard is made of wider pieces than laminboard.

Laminboard is one of the best materials of its type, but it is expensive. Most of the laminboard available is manufactured to high standards. It is used in places where a strong board material is required for solid construction, chiefly for the tops of tables where the design dictates long, unsupported lengths.

Blockboard is not a suitable base for veneered work as it is not sufficiently even across the surface. Its use results in a defect known as telegraphing. It may however be used successfully as a groundwork for lino, leather, or plastic laminates. Other than this its use is best confined to the bottoms of cabinets. The main problems encountered with blockboard are a result of an inferior standard of manufacture. Much of this material supplied has missing blocks, gaps where the blocks have not been pushed tightly together, and a poor surface through using badly peeled veneer.

☐ PARTICLE BOARD—CHIPBOARD

Chipboard is made from wood chips which are dried to a constant moisture content, and bonded together with synthetic resin under heat and pressure. It is available in different densities, the most dense being the best grade. Chipboard is obtainable with a plain or veneered surface. It is an excellent base for veneer but is rather heavy.

It is used chiefly as a material for solid construction and as such lends itself more readily to mass-production than to craftsmen-made items. It is a fairly stable material and good supplies of consistent quality are available. It is rather expensive and in many instances the home craftsman is better off buying solid timber. Although chipboard can be worked by hand it is difficult to groove and rebate as the wood is of a fairly stable nature. Dowel joints are the most practicable method of construction. Screws must not be overtightened or they will lose their holding power. A special screw with coarse thread is available for chipboard. When designing for this material remember that it is not a good structural material. A chipboard shelf, for instance, will require plenty of support as it can gradually sag under its own weight.

☐   PARTICLE BOARD—FLAXBOARD

Flaxboard is made from chemically treated flax shives, the residue of the flax plant after being divested of its linen fibres, mixed with synthetic resins and hot-pressed. The flax plant, which grows as a crop like oats or corn, is dried in the open after cutting and then transported to the factories for scutching. This is a beating process producing large numbers of small fine shives, which are hard in section, and from which all soft fibres are separated. The shives are graded so that the long ones may be further processed to make linen, whereas the shorter, less suitable fibres are used in the manufacture of cigarette paper. The remaining small shives are selected and the most suitable made into panels.

This is a board of increasing importance. It is lower in price than chipboard, and it has the advantage of lightness. It may be used, for instance, in the construction of wardrobe doors, which if too heavy can cause a light-weighted frame construction to overbalance.

☐   HARDBOARD

Hardboard is manufactured from pine logs, chipped, defibrated and felted by mechanical process into highly compressed rigid sheets. Its homogeneous construction makes it free from warping and other drawbacks common to laminated materials.

Hardboard has many uses, chiefly cladding or backing framed kitchen cabinets. It has an advantage over plywood where painting is required since it does not need sanding. Other uses include exhibition stands of peg board, toys, flush doors, picture frame and mirror backs. The thickness most commonly used is about $\frac{1}{8}$in (3mm) but $\frac{1}{4}$in (6mm) is also available.

Chapter 6

Materials

This chapter deals with the principal materials in their order of use. It is normal practice to clean up the inside and other inaccessible surfaces of the work with a smoothing plane, cabinet scraper, or glasspaper, then polish the inside surfaces before glueing the construction together. The outside can then be polished and the back can be screwed or nailed in place and all other fittings applied. Hence the order abrasives, finishes, glues, nails, screws and fittings.

ABRASIVES

Abrasives are part of the final finishing process. Once they have been used on the wood, cutting tools must not be reverted to as particles of abrasive embedded in the grain will quickly dull a sharp edged tool. To prepare a surface to a good finish clean it up first with a sharp, finely set smoothing plane. Make every effort to remove all tears with the plane, which will produce a better surface than that achieved by the heavy use of abrasive. If the wood is difficult cross-grain then use a scraper plane before succumbing to an abrasive. A cut surface will be sheer but an abraded surface will not possess the same sparkle because the fibres have been scrubbed back and forth. This is important when a transparent finish is to be applied.

☐ GLASSPAPER

The most common type of abrasive in use in the workshop is glasspaper. This is made by coating a stout paper with glue, and then, while the glue is still wet, sifting on finely powdered glass. This work is usually carried out in an electrostatic field so that the grains of glass are set on end. Various grades of fineness are obtainable, the first being called flour, then 0 (nought), 1, 1½, fine 2 (F2), middle 2 (M2), strong 2 (S2), and

(*left*) The Lervad instructors bench No 611 is of Scandinavian design and made from Danish beech. It stands 33½in (850mm) high and is fitted with 2 vices and a double row of bench dogs which are capable of holding work up to 72in (1.830m) long. To make the best of this bench it should be placed away from the wall and made rigid by screwing to the floor.

(*right*) Trinket box which can also be used for storing jewellery, cigars or coins. The original was made from solid mahogany with a teak veneer on the lid. The handle and lining were made from sycamore

(*above*) Flower trough. The original was made from solid mahogany and supported by legs made from parana pine; (*below*) coffee table of a traditional design. The original was made from solid mahogany. The top has an inlay of sycamore to decorate the edge

(*above*) Table with floating top of modern design and very serviceable as a coffee table. The underframe was made from Japanese oak and the blockboard top covered with Formica; (*below*) tea trolley. Wide rails produce strong joints and make this a very sturdy tea trolley. A curve on the underside of the rail gives elegance while large castors give manoeuverability

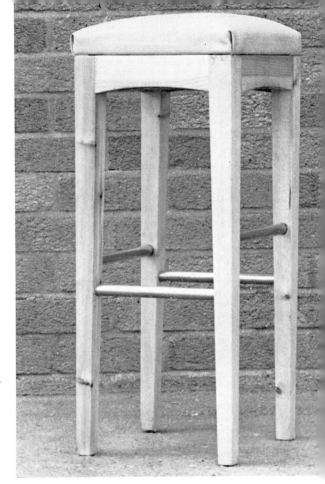

(right)
High stool. The lower
rails are set at three
different hights to
suit everybody

(left)
Small upholstered
stool. This is a strong
stool with many
uses. Dowel joints
make the framework
very easy to construct

$2\frac{1}{2}$. The smaller the number the finer the particles of glass used. For general use grades $1\frac{1}{2}$ and fine 2 are adequate.

The sheets are usually supplied 11in x 9in (280mm x 230mm) in size. Each sheet can be torn against a steel rule into 4 pieces. Glasspaper should be used wrapped around a cork block. This secures the paper and lengthens its life; it also increases the pressure that can be applied, and makes for a flatter surface. Always glasspaper with the grain when work is to be polished. For good results damp the wood to raise the grain then glasspaper flat.

☐ OTHER ABRASIVES

Other types of abrasives are Garnet, Aluminium oxide, and Silicon carbide. Any of these can be used for hand sanding but they are more commonly used when machine sanding. Garnet, which is a mineral, is crushed to form sharp individual grits. It is glued on to a paper backing in a similar fashion to glasspaper. Aluminium oxide (Al_2O_3) is a tough artificial abrasive. The grit is silver-grey in colour and is very hard. Silicon carbide (SiC), another artificial abrasive, is also very hard but brittle. All abrasive papers (except glasspaper) can be bought with the abrasive grains spread wide apart. This is called an open-coated paper and is recommended by the manufacturers for use on soft wood and when sanding gummy materials. For all other sanding, the close-coat type of paper is more satisfactory.

A paper recently introduced by the English Abrasives Corporation Ltd is called Lubrisil. This is a Silicon carbide paper which is stearate lubricated. This paper is non-clogging and will last at least twice as long as glasspaper. Type A lubrisil paper is preferred for hand sanding. Type C is for machine sanding. The grades recommended for hand sanding are 150 and 180. Store all abrasive papers away from any source of dampness or excessive heat and keep them in their original package until required.

A useful abrasive is fine wire wool grade 0000. This may be used for flattening down french polish or polyurethane varnish. If the surface is to be left semi-matt then wire wool will work into every hollow resulting in an even finish.

FINISHES

Finishes are applied to the wood to preserve the timber and to make the work look more attractive. If the pores of the wood are filled then the surface is easier to dust and keep clean.

☐   FRENCH POLISH

Polishing has always been a trade of its own, with special techniques and skills, but one of the interests of making one's own furniture is seeing the job through from beginning to end, and it is quite possible to produce a surface that is french polished to an adequate standard.

French polish is a traditional finish which still possesses considerable merit. It is easier to apply than the modern plastic type finishes, particularly when making individual items of furniture. It is neither heat resistant nor waterproof, but these two qualities are not required on the underframe of a coffee table or on the ends of a bed. A french polished table top has to be treated with care, but a plastic finished surface cannot be given unlimited rough treatment without showing signs of wear, and of the two finishes a french polished surface is much easier to repair. French polish must not be despised because we have modern alternatives; it has its own merits and disadvantages as have the modern finishes, and each must be taken into consideration before the craftsman makes a suitable choice.

Only two ingredients are used in the manufacture of french polish, shellac and industrial methylated spirit. Shellac is formed in the digestion process of the Laccifer Lacca insect which flourishes in certain provinces of India. It lives in colonies and feeds on tree sap. As the insect feeds a secretion is formed which eventually covers the whole swarm. This secretion hardens on contact with the air and it is collected for processing. The shellac is usually heated and then passed through a cloth screen which separates twigs and other impurities. Sometimes it is dissolved in industrial alcohol, which removes the trace of wax otherwise present in shellac. Transparent polish is made from bleached dewaxed lac, and is colourless as its name implies; alternatively white polish may be used, also made from bleached lac, but this is milky white in appearance. Button polish, another grade, has a deep yellowish tone. It is slightly cloudy and opaque, and is made from shellac which has not been dewaxed.

Transparent polish is recommended, being clear and harder than the other forms of polish. It can be obtained in liquid form, having been dissolved in industrial methylated spirit. Usually a little of this spirit will have to be used to thin the polish and make it a more watery consistency. Methylated spirit bought over the counter contains a blue dye. This can sully the colour of the polish but a little will do no harm.

After the surface of the work has been carefully prepared with the plane and perhaps a little glasspaper, brush on one thin coat of polish, working quickly, with a camel hair mop. Do not worry about bubbles in the polish as these soon disappear. Wait three minutes for the polish to dry, then lightly go over the work using flour grade glasspaper on the fingers. Do not use a cork block as the glasspaper must be worked into all the hollows. Brush on another *thin* coat, again working quickly. This will take a little longer to dry. Then gently flour paper the surface for the second time.

Some people complete the polishing at this stage with beeswax (see later in this chapter). If one requires more than a semi-matt finish then the work can be polished to a good shine as follows, though it is worth noting that the more shiny the surface the more easily all marks and blemishes can be seen.

Prepare a polishing pad from a small piece of non-fluffy cloth such as cotton or linen, containing a ball of cotton-wool about the size of a golf ball. Soak the cotton-wool in french polish, place this in the centre of the cloth and squeeze out as much as possible of the polish through the cloth. Now the polishing pad is ready charged and must be pulled over the surface of the work without scrubbing. Work very speedily in straight rows following the direction of the grain. The pad is working correctly if the surface dries almost instantly. Repeat this process several times, occasionally working the pad in tight circles across the work to spread the polish evenly. Gradually a really good shine will appear giving a very handsome finish. Should the pad stick during this process put a smear of linseed oil on the finger and apply this to the sole of the pad. Remember that one is not oiling the work but just lubricating the pad, so use only a trace of oil.

☐ WAX POLISH

Wax polish is probably the oldest method of applying a surface finish to an article. It is prepared from beeswax and turpentine. Pure beeswax is yellow in colour, but a white beeswax (bleached) can be obtained. The wax must be shredded and this can be easily done using a *Surform* tool. Cover the wax with best quality pure turpentine (not white spirit) and let the wax dissolve. This process can be speeded up by placing the container with the wax in hot water. Do not heat with a naked flame as turpentine is highly inflammable. The wax should be used in the form of a thin paste that is about the consistency of butter in the summer.

Beeswax should be applied with a soft cloth and rubbed well into the pores of the wood. This will produce a dull lustre suitable for the treatment of furniture and most indoor work. Beeswax is fairly soft and the finish can finger-mark. The polish can be hardened by the addition of carnauba wax (prepared from a Brazilian palm) in the proportion of about 1 part carnauba wax to three parts beeswax. Lighter fuel petrol is sometimes added to wax polish to speed up evaporation.

A proprietary brand of wax polish called *Briwax* can be used with excellent results. *Ronuk,* a non-sticky wax, is also useful for drawers and sliding parts.

☐ LINSEED OIL (AMER. FLAXSEED)

Linseed oil is prepared from the seed of the flax plant which is crushed to extract the oil. This oil dries slowly by absorbing oxygen from the air and forms an elastic film. When heated to about 200°C for several hours the linseed oil can absorb oxygen more rapidly. It is then known as boiled oil.

Linseed oil is applied to the wood as a preservative. It enriches the colour of the wood and for this reason is frequently used on oak and chestnut. Several applications are usually made with a rag, allowing drying intervals of a day between each coat.

Linseed oil can be mixed with an equal quantity of turpentine to form a kind of teak oil. Teak, being a greasy timber, takes a good oil finish.

☐ PAINT

A covering of paint protects the wood and gives a colourful appearance to the work. When carefully applied it can have a superior finish.

Glasspaper the work thoroughly to begin with. Work across the grain diagonally and finish with the grain. Brush on one coat of priming to seal the pores.

The next operation is to fill the pores with a thin paste called a filler; this will make the surface of the work level. The filler can be a plaster of paris type mixture such as *Alabastine* or *Polyfilla*. Work the filler across the panel with a painter's broad-knife. Allow 1 day for the filler to dry, glasspaper with a fine paper and cork block, then repeat the filling operation using the broad-knife with the grain. Allow another day for this to harden; then glasspaper the panel. The work should now be smooth and the grain completely filled. Inspect the work carefully and if the surface is not satisfactory repeat the filling operation a third time.

The work can now receive two applications of undercoat. The undercoat is the colour and bodying coat for the work. It is a flat finish (no gloss). Dust off the work using a rag slightly moistened with linseed oil. This tacky rag will pick up the dust but not apply linseed oil to the work. Using a worn but cared for brush, apply an even coat and feather off by letting the brush lightly touch the work. Travel across the panel, then diagonally, and finish lengthwise. Allow at least one day for this to dry thoroughly; then glasspaper, dust, and apply the second undercoat.

The top coat is the enamel or gloss coat and should be applied with the same care as the undercoat. If possible keep the work flat to prevent runs.

Maintain all brushes with thoroughness and care. Wash them out with white spirit and clean them with warm soapy water. Wrap brushes in paper to store them. Keep the paint in good condition by pouring sufficient quantity for the work in hand into a paint kettle and use it from there. Keep the tin sealed to avoid evaporation of the solvents.

☐ POLYURETHANE VARNISH

Polyurethane varnish is a hard plastic coating. It provides a transparent finish that can both enhance and protect the wood. This varnish is available in two different forms. Firstly the twin pack type which is generally recognised to be a tougher finish, but requires mixing immediately before use. Secondly the one pack type which is more straight forward to apply as it consists only of opening the tin and brushing the varnish straight onto the work. With this second type no mixing or stirring is required. Once the tin is re-sealed the contents will stay fresh for a long period.

Polyurethane varnish can be applied similarly to paint; that is to say for best results on hardwood a grain filler should be used which is compatible with the varnish and of the same colour as the wood. Apply the filler and leave to set overnight before rubbing down with fine glasspaper (flour). Remove all dust with a tacky rag and then flow one coat of varnish onto the work with a brush. Some people prefer to thin this first coat with the thinners recommended by the manufacturer in order to gain maximum penetration. There is usually a time limit with this type of varnish at which stage the surface must be rubbed down and the next coat applied. Working beyond this time limit can have disastrous results.

The final coat must be allowed to harden for several days and then it can be flatted with fine glasspaper or grade 0000 wirewool. Alternatively good results can be obtained by using an electric finishing sander (not a rotary disc sander) with fine aluminium oxide paper. The surface should not be cut through to the bare wood, but it can be flatted to a smooth, even finish. This will provide a matt surface akin to ground glass. It may be left like this or it can be polished using either liquid metal polish such as *Brasso*, or a special polyurethane polishing cream. This will result in a high gloss and excellent finish.

As with all products, read the manufacturer's instructions carefully before starting the work.

☐ TANALISED TIMBER

Tanalith C, a preservative, is suitable for the treatment of outdoor woodwork. It is forced into timber by a vacuum/pressure impregnating plant at a pressure of 180lb per sq in. Chemicals which are naturally present in the wood react with Tanalith C to make it water insoluble. The water content of the preservative dries out in the air and the preservative salts remain fixed in the timber.

This treatment imparts a soft greenish colour to the wood and looks attractive as it blends well with natural surroundings. Tanalised timber can be painted if so desired and may be glued in the normal way. Tanalised timber is exceedingly durable. Treated pine fencing has a life of well over thirty years.

☐ FORMICA

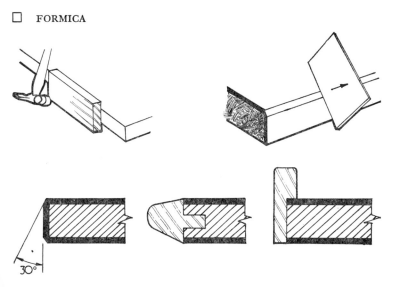

Fig 85 Methods of edge lipping plastic laminate. The edge of plastic laminate is unattractive and requires concealing. Self edging can be performed as shown. Trim to 30° with a cabinet scraper or block plane.
Edging strips made of hardwood can make attractive alternatives

Formica is basically a plastic laminate. It consists of three layers of paper impregnated with resin and bonded together under great pressure and high temperature. The first layer is the base paper. Over this is placed a white or coloured sheet on which the pattern has been printed. The top layer is a cellulose paper which becomes transparent during the curing process in manufacture, and forms a protective skin. This skin will resist heat, impact, abrasion and staining. All laminates emerge with a glossy surface, but where a matt surface is required sheets are dull rubbed with a fine abrasive at the factory. The laminate is 1/16in (1.6mm) thick. It is easier to apply than veneer and does not require polishing. It is widely used as wall panelling and working surfaces, and has very special advantages in kitchen areas.

The technique of cutting, trimming and applying Formica is not difficult to master. It can be cut by circular saw. A high peripheral speed is required, so use the biggest saw blade the saw bench can accommodate. A fine tooth saw is essential since it reduces the amount of finishing required. Cut the sheet with the decorative face upwards, making sure that it is held firmly down to the table. Portable electric saws may be used. The rotation of these saws demands that the sheet should be cut from the back to avoid broken edges. Travelling saws are the most convenient way to cut, since the sheet is held firmly while the saw moves across the work. It is most likely that the local supplier will have this type of saw. Add $\frac{1}{4}$in (6mm), for overhang, to the sizes required, and let the supplier do the work of cutting; this way one can usually buy 'off-cuts' at a cheaper price.

Laminates can be cut by hand. Use a fine toothed tenon saw at a low angle. Mark lines on the surface of the sheet with a soft pencil, these being easily removed later with soap and water. Take care to support the sheet to prevent splitting. Alternatively a Stanley trimming knife fitted with the purpose-made blade can be used for cutting the laminate. Lay the sheet on a firm base, decorative face upwards, score the surface about five times using the Stanley knife against a thin straight edge, then keeping pressure on the straight edge, lift the off-cut side gently. The sheet will start to break along the scribed cut.

When using Formica the core material (groundwork) should be chipboard, blockboard or plywood. Solid timber is not suitable due to its movement. As with normal veneered work, the panels should be counter-veneered. This is achieved by balancing the work by another sheet of laminate of the same thickness bonded to the back of the core. For this purpose the manufacturers produce backing boards which are considerably cheaper than the standard laminate. Counterveneering is essential for free-standing panels such as doors, but is not necessary if the work is to be secured to a solid carcase or wall cladding.

Synthetic resin adhesives (Cascamite, Aerolite, etc) are the most successful bonding agents, having good heat and water resistance, but they do need sustained pressure whilst setting takes place. For this reason synthetic rubber-based adhesives (Bostik, Evostik, etc) are often more suitable. These adhesives, though generally more expensive, are able to stick on touch without sustained pressure, but in certain conditions of heat and humidity they too can be unsuitable. Therefore, if in doubt it is better to use a synthetic resin glue.

When working with the synthetic rubber adhesive, spread a thin film of the adhesive onto both contacting surfaces and wait twenty minutes. By this time the adhesive will appear touch dry. It is important to place the laminate on the core material accurately as once touched down it has no opportunity to slide. Location can be done by locating pins at 3 corners, or by sandwiching a sheet of brown paper between the work. The paper will not stick but it allows one to locate the work accurately, then the paper may be withdrawn, allowing the surfaces to meet. Take care to avoid trapping air.

Careful consideration should be given to the finish of edges, not only for reasons of appearance, but also because it is vital if resistance to wear and abrasion is to be maintained. One of the most successful methods is self-edging with laminate. The laminate can be applied slightly over-size and then trimmed down to the surface finish. Trimming can be done quickly with a power router, or with a low angle block plane. The bevel angle should be about 30° to the perpendicular as this gives less emphasis to the dark core line. A final finish can be given using a cabinet scraper.

When using contact adhesives the core edges should be given two coats, the second coat being applied after the first has dried. After applying the edging make sure it is firmly fixed by tapping with a block of wood and hammer.

Various extruded metal mouldings with plastic inserts are

I

available. These are particularly suitable for kitchen furniture.

Laminated plastic provides a colourful and hardwearing
surface, though it does have limitations; it can be cut by sharp
knives and worn out by abrasion. The surface should be
cleaned with a damp rag; never use furniture polish as this
will in time form a grimy layer and spoil the appearance. Do
not iron directly onto the laminate but protect the surface
with a thick blanket of cloth. Similarly do not place hot dishes
straight from the oven onto a Formica surface. When using a
hand mincing machine always place a pad between the screw
and the table edge. Alcohol, soft drinks, tea or coffee will not
affect Formica, but take care with strong chemicals such as
caustic soda, hydrogen peroxide, lavatory cleaner and washing
bleach, as these can affect the surface.

GLUES

☐ ANIMAL GLUE—SCOTCH GLUE

Scotch glue, which is the traditional glue of the cabinet
maker, is still derived from abattoir waste. The dry glue is usually sold in pearl form and is prepared in the workshop using
a double container. The glue placed in the inner container
is heated by water held in the outer container. The water
does not exceed 100°C so the glue will not burn. Thermo-
statically controlled electric pots are obtainable.

Fill the inner pot one-third with pearl glue and top up with
cold water. Stir once every two minutes for at least ten minutes. The pearls will swell and stirring prevents them forming
a lump which would be slow to dissolve.

It takes about half an hour to prepare the glue. When ready
it should flow in a continuous, thin, unbroken stream from
the brush; it should make a spattering noise when it falls onto
the glue in the pot; it should feel sticky between the fingers
as it begins to gel.

When using Scotch glue always make sure the room is
warm, close all windows and keep the glue pot in the water
jacket to maintain the glue at the correct temperature. Work
quickly.

Always cramp up before glueing. This will set the cramps to size and ensure there are no hidden snags. Take the work apart, glue up and cramp up for the second time. Glued work should be left cramped until the next day. This allows the glue to harden.

Scotch glue is not waterproof, it takes time to prepare and some form of heating—either gas ring or electric glue pot—is essential; it is not the glue for an ambitious assembly job requiring time in the glueing up stage, as it chills easily.

However, although rather out of favour at the present time, this is a good glue, being very strong, seldom staining the wood, and surplus glue can be easily removed from the corners of the work with hot water. Scotch glue forms a bond between two porous materials by soaking into the pores and setting like little dowels. This explains why the glue may be used successfully only on materials such as wood, leather or hessian. It will not stick glass, plastic or metal.

☐   ANIMAL GLUE—CASEIN GLUE (eg casco)

Casein glue is manufactured from skimmed milk, which has a 3% casein content. It is usually supplied in dry powder form and is mixed with water following the instructions on the tin.

Casein glue must be stored dry and sealed against contact with carbon dioxide in the air. There is a tendency for this glue to stain so its use is generally confined to the building industry. It must also be realised that this glue is not sticky, so cramps must be used until the glue sets hard.

However, it is easy to prepare, is used cold, and has good resistance to moisture. It will bond wood to linoleum, Formica, cardboard, paper, cloth, leather and cork.

☐   SYNTHETIC RESIN GLUES

Mineral Glues—Polyvinyl Acetate (eg Casco PVA, Extra Bond, Resin W) One of the more recent glues is called polyvinyl acetate emulsion glue, or PVA for short. This glue has the components of coke and lime. PVA glue is obtained in liquid form, as an emulsion, that is minute particles of PVA are dispersed in water. It is a very swift gripping glue on porous materials. As the water is quickly absorbed this has the effect of forcing the particles of resin together until they unite and form a firm bond.

The disadvantages of PVA are that it must not be allowed to freeze in storage or it will coagulate and cannot be reconstituted. Similarly, it must be worked at normal room temperature for the best results.

The advantages of PVA are that it requires no mixing, it is fairly waterproof, colourless, and has a certain amount of natural flexibility. The last is a good point, as many modern glues dry hard to the extent of being brittle. In all respects PVA makes a very good substitute for Scotch glue and is probably the best type of wood adhesive for the home craftsman. It will glue everything except rubber, PVC and polythene.

Urea Formaldehyde (eg Cascamite, Aerolite 300) This glue is produced by the reaction of Ammonia with Carbon Dioxide and Formaldehyde. If the process were continued until saturation it would produce a solid but brittle glass-like substance. For the manufacture of glue the process is only partly completed, and by the addition of a hardener which is a catalyst the reaction is completed in the joint. A joint glued in this way is very strong and highly resistant to water, heat and bacteria. This is the most suitable type of glue for boat building and all outdoor work and can be used for Formica work.

Urea formaldehyde adhesives are available in two forms, separate resin and hardener or powder form with hardener added.

☐   CONTACT ADHESIVES (eg Evostik, Bostik, Superstik)
This is a synthetic rubber adhesive and is formed as a by-product of the petroleum industry.

A thin, even film of adhesive should be applied to both surfaces and allowed to touch dry (about 20mins). Then the two surfaces are pressed together over the whole bond area, hand pressure usually being sufficient. This glue is suitable only for butt jointing operations and cannot be used where joints have to be slid into place, eg mortise and tenon joints, dovetails, etc. Impact adhesives will glue most materials, but are not suitable for expanded polystyrene.

NAILS

Nails are used as a quick method of fastening pieces of wood together, but they are not as strong as screws, nor as easy to remove.

Special types of nail are available according to the job in hand. The round wire nail is the most common; it has a large head which is easy to hit and may be put in flush with the surface of the work. If the nail is outsize the ends can be clenched round underneath to make a firmer job. Staggering the nails can prevent splitting. The oval nail has only a small head and can be punched below the surface of the work, the resulting holes being filled with putty and painted over, or filled with solid beeswax, glasspapered over and polished in the normal way. Oval nails may be placed with the grain and this reduces the chance of splitting the wood. Panel pins are very thin and may be used on small work such as boxes and picture frames. They may be punched below the surface and are easy to conceal. The clout nail is used for fixing roofing felt; it has a large head which secures the felt firmly and reduces the risk of tearing. The tack is the upholsterer's method of fixing fabric and webbing. It is available in sizes from $\frac{3}{8}$in (10mm) to $\frac{3}{4}$in (20mm) and can be ordered as either ordinary or improved. The improved type has the larger head and under the head are two small lugs which secure the webbing or fabric when the tack is hit firmly home. A good tack is sharp and stands up with little pressure. A sprig is a small nail used for holding pictures in a frame. It is usually inserted with the side of a large chisel acting as a hammer.

SCREWS

There are three head shapes in common use. The countersink screw is used when the head of the screw must finish flush with the surface of the work, the raised countersink may be used for a more pleasing appearance, and the roundhead is generally used for fastening metal to wood with the exception of hinges which are always fitted with countersink screws.

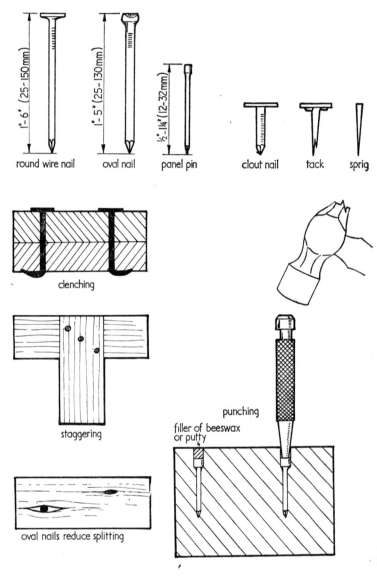

round wire nail   oval nail   panel pin   clout nail   tack   sprig

1"- 6" (25 - 150mm)

1"- 5" (25 - 130mm)

½"- 1¼" (12 - 32mm)

clenching

staggering

oval nails reduce splitting

punching

filler of beeswax
or putty

Fig 86   Types of nails

These three types of screw may be turned by either a slot or a pozidriv recess.

The pozidriv, a recent improvement in the form of recess, has four major advantages over the slotted type head. The primary advantage is that the screwdriver cannot slip. This reduces accidental damage and brings about increased effici-

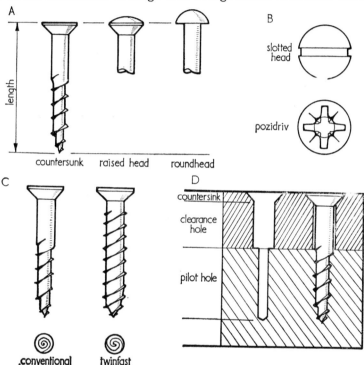

Fig 87 Types of screws: (*a*) types of screw head (*b*) method of driving (*c*) types of thread and (*d*) fitting a countersink screw

ency. The second advantage is that the same screwdriver will fit both large and small screws. This reduces the handling time and means fewer tools are required for the job. The third benefit is that the screw is always aligned with the screwdriver. Finally, the pozidriv screw tends to look more decorative than the slotted head, though this is a matter of personal opinion.

There are two principal types of thread. The pozidriv twinfast woodscrew is designed for use in low density chipboard, blockboard, fibreboard and softwoods. This screw has a two-start thread which offers increasing holding power, and because it buries two thread pitches each turn this screw can be inserted almost twice as quickly as the conventional screw. The twinfast screw is also threaded nearly to the head. The relieved shank eliminates wedge action and minimises splitting.

☐ FITTING A COUNTERSINK SCREW

The position for the screw should be marked on the wood with a centre punch to prevent the drill wandering. A drill must be selected which is just bigger than the shank of the screw. The following table is helpful:

Gauge of screw	Clearance hole in (mm)	Pilot hole in (mm)
4	$\frac{1}{8}$ (3)	5/64 (2)
6	5/32 (4)	5/64 (2)
8	3/16 (5)	3/32 (2.5)
10	7/32 (5.5)	$\frac{1}{8}$ (3)
12	$\frac{1}{4}$ (6)	$\frac{1}{8}$ (3)

The clearance hole is drilled followed by the countersink which must be of sufficient depth to allow the head of the screw to fit flush. No countersink is required on softwoods. A pilot hole is usually drilled to take the core of the screw thread. This eases insertion of the screw and a lubricant of soap or vaseline will assist further without loss of holding power. In hardwoods, such as oak, where owing to the acid nature of the timber brass screws are always used, preferably a steel screw is first inserted to cut a thread. This will help to prevent the softer brass screw breaking.

Screws are available in a variety of metals and finishes. The commonest metal is steel, which is strong and suitable for most ordinary applications. Brass screws are less strong but offer medium corrosion resistance and look well on furniture. Stainless steel is used for good resistance to corrosion. Silicon bronze screws are used for marine applications and aluminium alloy screws are used with aluminium fittings. In general it is good practice to use screws of the same material as the metal fittings they are to accompany.

Certain finishes can be applied to screws either to make them more decorative or to protect them from weathering. These finishes are listed with descriptions and suggested uses.

Steel *plus* —

Bright zinc plate	Bright attractive protective coating	All dry interior uses and with a paint finish outdoors
Sheradised (zinc)	Dull grey protective coat; may turn brown	Most exterior uses on buildings; good surface for painting
Nickel plate	Bright reflective finish; may tarnish	Dry interior fasteners, eg shelves
Chromium plate	Attractive bright reflective finish	Fairly dry interior work in kitchens and bathroom
Brass plate (electro-brass)	Reflective bright yellow finish	Furniture for matching against brass; dry interior work only
Bronze metal antique	Dark brown finish	Interior use with oxidised copper fittings
Dark florentine bronze	Near black finish	Interior use with oxidised copper fittings
Antique copper bronze	Uniform bronze colour	Interior use with copper, bronze and matching timber finishes
Black japanned	Overall black enamel	General interior use; must be re-painted outdoors for protection
Berlin blacked	Overall dull black enamel	General interior use; must be re-painted outdoors for protection

When ordering wood screws the following information is required:

1 Quantity: screws are usually sold singly, by the dozen, or by the gross
2 Length
3 Diameter by screw gauge: a number 8 screw is a general size. For thinner use number 6, or for stouter number 10
4 Material or finish
5 Type of head: eg 10 $1\frac{1}{2}$in (38mm) No 8 pozidriv countersink head screws

HINGES

☐ TYPES OF HINGES

Figure 88 shows a best quality butt hinge made from extruded brass. The knuckle is solid and therefore very strong. Such a hinge will always have an uneven number of knuckles, generally five. The plate with three knuckles is fastened to the cabinet side and the plate with two knuckles to the door. This is the strongest method of fitting this type of hinge. Brass hinges will always be fitted with brass countersink screws. The pin in the hinge may be either brass or steel. Such a hinge is expensive but good quality work deserves good quality fittings.

Common sizes are		
$1\frac{1}{4}$in x	$\frac{7}{8}$in	38mm x 22mm
2 in x	$1\frac{1}{8}$in	51mm x 29mm
$2\frac{1}{2}$in x	$1\frac{3}{8}$in	63mm x 35mm
3 in x	$1\frac{5}{8}$in	76mm x 41mm
4 in x	$2\frac{3}{8}$in	101mm x 60mm

A poorer quality hinge is made from folded brass. This is cheaper but less strong and can usually be distinguished by an even number of knuckles.

Common sizes are		
1 in x	$\frac{1}{2}$in	25mm x 12mm
$1\frac{1}{4}$in x	$\frac{5}{8}$in	32mm x 16mm
$1\frac{1}{2}$in x	$\frac{3}{4}$in	38mm x 19mm
2 in x	1 in	51mm x 25mm
$2\frac{1}{2}$in x	$1\frac{1}{4}$in	63mm x 32mm
3 in x	$1\frac{1}{2}$in	76mm x 38mm
4 in x	2 in	101mm x 51mm

Such hinges may also be obtained in chromium plate.

The backflap hinge (fig 88c) is used for work such as the drop leaf on a table.

The piano hinge (fig 88D) is used for piano lids and work of a similar nature requiring an extra long hinge. A usual size is 36in x 1in (915mm x 25mm).

The strap hinge (fig 88E) is obtainable in natural brass with a steel pin. Open sizes: $\frac{3}{8}$in x $1\frac{7}{8}$in (10mm x 47), 7/16in x $2\frac{3}{8}$in (11mm x 60mm).

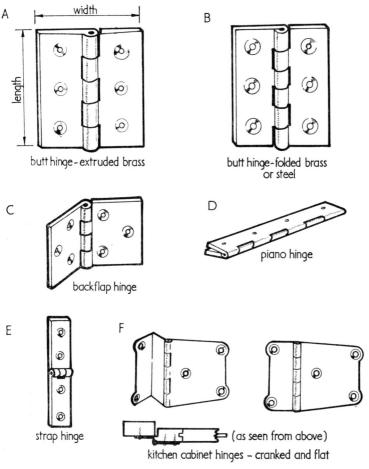

butt hinge-extruded brass

butt hinge-folded brass or steel

backflap hinge

piano hinge

strap hinge

kitchen cabinet hinges – cranked and flat

(as seen from above)

Fig 88 Types of hinges

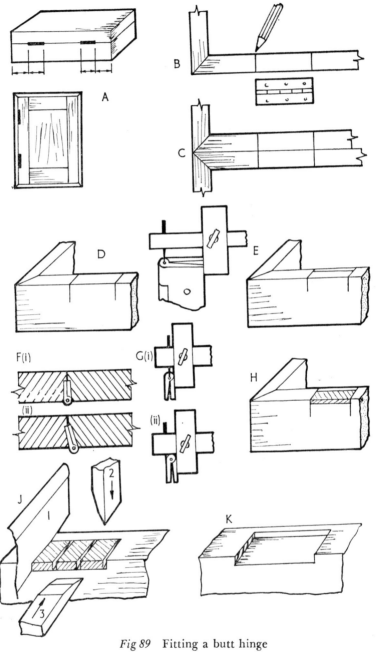

Fig 89 Fitting a butt hinge

Kitchen cabinet hinges are extremely useful. These are surface fitting and the cranked type may be used on a framed
and rebated door (fig 88F).

☐   FITTING A BUTT HINGE
  A On a box allow the length of the hinge in from the ends.
     For a door it is usual to allow a little more space under
     the bottom hinge.
  B Mark the exact length of the hinge on the work in pencil.
  C Transfer these marks to the lid and square across with a
     try square and pencil.
  D Partly square these pencil marks onto the adjoining sur-
     face, where the butt of the hinge has to be let in.
  E Set a marking gauge to half the width of the hinge, as
     shown, and gauge the hinge positions from the outside of
     the box.
  F There are two methods of fitting a hinge:
       i The hinge is let equally into both parts of the job.
          This is the method shown for the box in figure 89A.
      ii The knuckle of the hinge is let entirely into the mov-
          ing part. This method is shown on the cabinet in figure
          89A. It can result in a better final appearance as the
          line of the carcase is not broken visually.
  G Depending on the method of hinging used, set a marking
     gauge to either one-half the thickness of the hinge
     knuckle, or to the full thickness.
  H Gauge for the thickness of the hinge, then knife in the
     pencil lines where required.
  J Saw across the fibres for as much of the way as is possible,
     and remove the waste with a chisel.
  K The completed recess will have a sloping base to suit the
     flap of the hinge. Fit the hinge with the centre screw
     only. Adjust this as necessary by pelleting the hole
     (levering the fibres across with a bradawl). When correct
     insert the other screws.

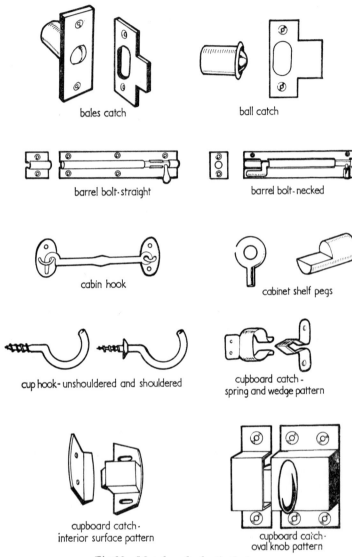

bales catch

ball catch

barrel bolt-straight

barrel bolt-necked

cabin hook

cabinet shelf pegs

cup hook-unshouldered and shouldered

cupboard catch-
spring and wedge pattern

cupboard catch-
interior surface pattern

cupboard catch-
oval knob pattern

Fig 90 Metal and plastic fittings

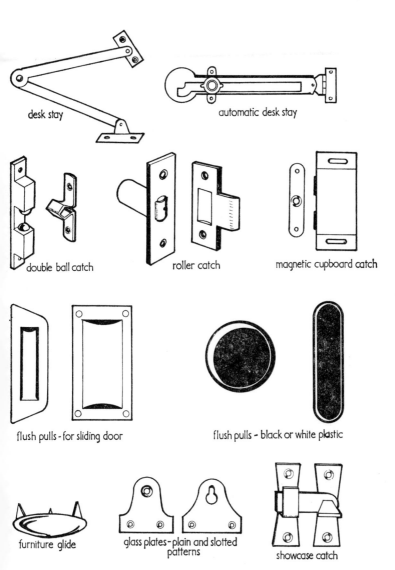

desk stay

automatic desk stay

double ball catch

roller catch

magnetic cupboard catch

flush pulls - for sliding door

flush pulls - black or white plastic

furniture glide

glass plates - plain and slotted patterns

showcase catch

FITTINGS

Good quality fittings are becoming increasingly difficult to buy. Not only are they more scarce but also more expensive; however, the best workmanship requires the very best materials. Sometimes plastic goods are neat, strong and well made, but generally fittings manufactured from solid brass look better. Solid brass fittings, not to be confused with brassed fittings, should be carefully polished.

☐ CASTORS

The purpose of any castor is to make heavy furniture mobile. One of the most successful designs has been the ball type castor invented by George Shepherd, an Australian. The product was brought to England and manufactured by Archibald Kenrick and Sons Ltd, the first Shepherd castor being marketed in 1950.

The benefits of a ball type castor over the old-fashioned type are improved socket fitting, no need for lubrication, exceptional long life, and good castoring action. Criticisms are that the castor is too mobile; therefore furniture may be moved around so often that a pathway is made on the floor covering.

There are two main ways of fixing a castor. The plate fixing requires four holes to be made in the woodwork with a brad-awl. Four screws pass through these holes to secure the castor. The alternative method of fixing, usually more convenient, is the socket and peg type. A hole must be drilled $\frac{3}{8}$in (10mm) in diameter and $1\frac{1}{4}$in (32mm) deep. The socket is pushed into the hole and tapped home with a hammer. The stem of the castor is inserted into the socket and pushed firmly home.

Since the introduction of the Shepherd castor the traditional wheel type castor has been improved. A wheel castor was chosen, because of its elegant looks, for the tea trolley described in chapter 9.

MASONRY WALL FIXING

Wall fixings can be made by putting a screw into a plastic

or fibre plug inserted into a pre-drilled hole. The screw expands the plug against the sides of the hole, making a firm fixing.

Care must be taken to drill a hole the correct size for the plug and the screw. Generally a number 8 screw is fitted into a number 8 plug and the hole is drilled with a number 8 masonry drill. Wall plugs of the plastic type will usually fit screws of three different gauges but may require a larger size drill.

A masonry drill, though similar in appearance to a morse drill, has a hard metal insert of tungsten carbide to form the cutting edge. The bit must be turned at slow speed, using either a hand drill or slow running electric drill. Drills turning faster than 1000 revolutions per minute can cause the masonry bit to overheat, resulting in the hard steel edge coming adrift.

The plain shank of the screw must not enter the plug, as it can cause the screw to seize and break at the thread to shank junction. A depth stop can be provided for the drill by wrapping sticky tape around the drill. This way the plug may be made to sink $\frac{1}{8}$in (3mm) below the surface of the wall.

Long battens can be fitted by securing the ends firmly to the wall. Further plugs and screws can be inserted by drilling directly through the batten into the wall behind with the one masonry bit. The spiral twist of the masonry bit will withdraw all dust from the hole. A plug of the fibre type can then be inserted and pushed to the bottom of the hole with the screw. This avoids all difficulties of locating the hole in the batten with the hole in the wall. Remember too that a little lubricant of vaseline or soap will help the screw to enter easily.

A fairly recent innovation is the masonry nail. This is made from hardened steel and has a specially shaped point. Take care to choose the correct size of nail for the job in hand by reading the manufacturer's instructions. These nails are hard but brittle and can 'fly'. Wear protective goggles to shield the eyes when working.

K

Chapter 7

Woodworking Machinery

THE PURPOSE OF MACHINERY

Not so long ago the machine was thought to be of no benefit to the craftsman working in wood. It was believed that craft items should be made entirely by hand. It was argued that machines were expensive, that the same work could always be done by simple hand tools, and that the use of machinery dictated a poor design, being planned around the machine to the detriment of the final product.

Nowadays most people will accept the machine as part of the workshop situation, having realised it can save time and effort. Machines will help with laborious chores such as sawing the length of a plank or cutting out several rails from one wide board. Work can be tackled in minutes by a circular saw which would take hours by hand.

SAFETY

All tools are safer when they are sharp. Learn how to maintain every machine tool in your workshop, thereby keeping them in prime condition. Many people buy a circular saw without knowing how to sharpen the blade; pushing against a blunt circular saw causes the majority of machine accidents.

When setting up a machine it is often necessary to place the hands near the moving parts, so isolate the machine before making adjustments. Apart from the push button switch on the machine there should be an isolator switch on the wall. This may be a fuse box type switch which can be turned to OFF, or it may be a plug and socket, in which case switch off the socket and REMOVE THE PLUG. One can then adjust the machine in complete safety.

Certain other precautions can also be taken. Belt drives must be guarded as must all revolving parts. It should be made quite difficult, if not impossible, to get fingers near to anything that turns at speed. Furthermore, the machine should be securely fixed either to the floor or to a solid bench; there should be no possibility of it toppling over in use. When a machine has been set up check the revolving parts, see that they can turn freely and make sure all nuts are tight before switching on.

Loose clothing should not be worn; ties are a particular hazard and should be either removed or tucked securely into the shirt. A good workshop smock without loose cuffs or dangling strings will protect clothes. If the machine creates swarf in the direction of the operator wear an eye shield as protection (appendix B).

All machinery can be divided into two basic types, fixed and portable. Both types should be made safe electrically and must be earthed (grounded). However, portable machinery is the more dangerous from this point of view as it can be carried into new and potentially dangerous situations. This particularly applies to the electric drill. This tool is only as safe as its insulation and as the earthing (grounding) of the socket. One assumes that every socket is earthed efficiently but this is not necessarily the case. A fault can occur, such as metal swarf entering the rubber lead and causing a drill to become live. In this event only a good earth connection will prevent electricity flowing through the body to the ground. There are three main ways of preventing an electrical accident.

1. Make sure the drill is efficiently earthed and when working stand on a wooden floor or in rubber boots. On no account hold onto a metal water pipe or gas pipe.

2. The safest method is to reduce the voltage (as in the USA) to no greater than 115 volts, using a step down transformer. This should employ a centre tapped earthed connection, then either lead will supply about 55 volts to the drill. The transformer should be wired with a short flex to the mains supply and a long working flex to supply current at low voltage to the drill (plate 4).

3. The cheapest method of ensuring electrical safety is to use only a double insulated tool. This is signified by the symbol of one square inside another stamped on the tool, as on the Stanley Bridges XK 360. This is a glass filled nylon

bodied drill. Even the metal chuck is insulated from the armature of the drill. This form of insulation will not protect the operator should the lead be cut but in all other respects it has a high degree of safety.

CIRCULAR SAW

The circular saw is obtainable either as a bench or a portable machine. It is known by the largest diameter of saw blade it will take.

☐   THE BENCH MACHINE

All circular saws should be provided with sufficient power for the blade to perform its normal quota of work without protest. The rule of thumb is to allow one horsepower for every inch (25mm) depth of cut. It must be realised that circular saws require a lot of power to work effectively.

The power is usually transmitted to the saw spindle by means of a v belt. This is similar to the fan belt of a car. On larger machines two or even three belts are fitted in order to transmit adequate power from the motor to the blade. These belts need no attention. On no account should they be fitted spring tight.

The motor is seldom connected directly to the blade. Only on smaller saws, usually fitted as attachments to an electric drill, is the saw blade fitted directly to an extension of the motor. The reason for this is that circular saws have to revolve at a certain speed for optimum efficiency and seldom does this speed comply with the speed of the motor.

Tensioning is required with circular saw blades as with handsaws. Without tension the rim of the blade becomes slack at speed. The blades are usually tensioned to suit a peripheral speed of 10,000ft per minute (50 metres per second). The table below gives the approximate spindle speed of the machine against the diameter of the saw blade.

Speeds of Circular Saws

Diameter of saw		Approximate spindle speed (peripheral speed 10,000ft per minute)
in	mm	rev/min
6	150	6,370
8	200	4,770
10	250	3,820
12	300	3,185

Saws not designed for these normal applications have to be specially tensioned to suit the speed of rotation.

When ordering a circular saw blade the following information is usually required:

1 The type of saw—this is normally a plate saw but other saws, eg hollow ground, swage, are obtainable for special purposes.
2 Diameter of saw.
3 Size of centre hole to suit machine spindle.
4 Type of tooth—rip saw, crosscut saw or combination shape. This is dictated by the timber that is to be cut.
5 The spindle speed.

All bench circular saws have some means of adjusting the amount of blade that shows above the table. On cheaper machines it is usual to have a rise-and-fall table. More expensive machines have a rise-and-fall saw arbour which is better as it means the operator is always working at a constant table height, usually about 34in (860mm). The reason for adjusting the depth of cut is not only to make it possible to saw grooves and rebates but also to enable the saw to be set so that the upper surface of the timber is just penetrated by the blade. It will be found that the circular saw will cut more smoothly in this set-up as more teeth are engaged (fig 91). Frequently

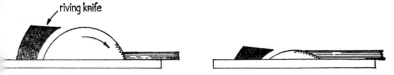

Fig 91 Use of rise-and-fall arbour. When the saw is set low in the table, more teeth are in engagement with the work. This results in smoother cutting

the saw blade can be adjusted on the machine to operate at any angle from 90° to 45° with respect to the table. This allows bevel cuts to be performed. The more expensive machines have a tilting arbour (saw spindle), whilst cheaper machines are fitted with tilting tables.

It is desirable to have some means of crosscutting accurately. Often a longitudinal slot is provided in the table to take a simple mitring and crosscutting fence. This is satisfactory for small work but for anything large it is usual to prepare a suitable wooden jig.

The ripping fence should be adjustable not only across the table but also to and from the blade. When used for ripping and deep sawing the fence should guide the work only to the blade. The leading edge of the fence should project about half the gullet depth of the saw and should be shaped to the approximate curve of the blade. This prevents the wood binding between the fence and the saw blade. The latter would cause loss of power and could result in the work being thrown back at the operator. When crosscutting it is more convenient to have the fence extended to the full depth of the table. For those saws fitted with a long and non-adjustable fence a false timber plate can normally be attached with machine screws.

Certain timbers, notably elm, will pinch on the saw blade once the cut has been started. To prevent this happening and to keep the cut open a riving knife is fitted directly behind the blade. The riving knife should be of a thickness equal to the kerf of the saw.

The circular saw is the most dangerous woodworking machine; hence the need for certain safety precautions. Firstly, the blade should be well protected. It should be guarded underneath the table by the cabinet and above the table there should be a special (crown) blade guard. This can be a metal shield attached to the riving knife. Alternatively a spring guard is fitted which encloses the teeth of the saw and only opens as wood is fed through. Always use a push stick (a stick of wood notched at one end) when working near the teeth of a saw; it matters little if the push stick gets sawn in half. Oil the machine little and often and make sure it works as efficiently as possible. The fence should work easily and so should the rise-and-fall mechanism.

☐ THE PORTABLE MACHINE

There are times when it is easier to take the saw to the work than the work to the saw, for example when sawing large panels. It is easier to place the panel on trestles and cut with the portable saw rather than man-handle the timber to a bench machine which will require at least double the amount of operating space.

The portable saw may be regarded as a powered handsaw, its chief uses being ripping and crosscutting. It is essential that the work is held securely. A satisfactory method is to set the depth of cut to just greater than the thickness of the material being sawn. A waste batten may then be placed under the work and the saw arranged to cut through the work and into the batten. This prevents the sawn off piece of timber from dropping down at the completion of the cut.

☐ SHARPENING A CIRCULAR SAW

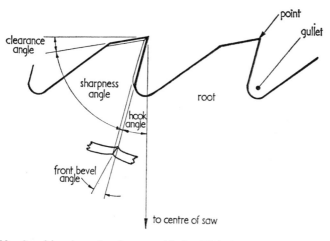

Fig 92 Combination circular saw blade. This is the typical type of blade that is supplied as an electric drill attachment. Clearance angle 10°, sharpness angle 65°, hook angle 15°, top bevel 5°, front bevel 10° and set 0.015 in

An ordinary circular saw blade (not tungsten tipped) requires sharpening about every four hours of use.

1 Before removing it from the machine lower the blade so

that the teeth are level with the table. Whilst the saw is running, place an oilstone on the table to just touch the points of the teeth. This will cause sparks but will level all the teeth and produce a guide to sharpening.

2　Remove the blade from the machine and secure it in the vice between two circular pieces of wood a little smaller than the blade. A bolt through the middle will hold everything together.

3　With a millsaw file sharpen every tooth which is set *away* (alternate teeth) by (a) filing across the top with the handle about 5° below the horizontal, until the topping mark has just disappeared; (b) three strokes of the file in the gullet of the saw, working on the leading edge of the tooth at an angle of about 10° from the square position. Such a blade will then rip and crosscut and is called a combination blade. Should the blade only be required for ripping then sharpen the leading edge of each tooth at 0° (ie parallel to the axis).

About every sixth time of sharpening the blade will require setting. This can be done with a pliers-type saw set suitable for circular saw. Alternatively, and very easily, the teeth may be hammer set by placing the saw on a metal block with one corner chamfered to about 5°. Hit the top half of the alternate teeth with a hammer, then reverse the blade and repeat for the other side.

Saw blades are obtainable coated with *teflon*. This is fused onto the blade at 400° C and is quite permanent. The advantage of this type of blade is that the coating both reduces friction and prevents the blade from rusting.

BANDSAW

The bandsaw has a blade that is an endless ribbon of steel with teeth shaped on the leading edge. The blade can be ⅛in (3mm) to 7in (180mm) in width, depending upon the size of the machine. Generally in the home workshop the blade is no more than ⅜in (10mm) wide. The narrower the blade the tighter the curve the bandsaw is capable of cutting. The blade revolves around two large pulleys. The top pulley is free wheeling whereas the bottom pulley is powered by an electric motor. A bandsaw suitable for a large woodworking machine shop can have pulley wheels up to 60in (1.5m) in diameter. Some smaller machines have wheels that are only 10in (250mm) in diameter. The maximum distance for a cut into a board (the throat size) can never be greater than the diameter of the wheel on a two-wheel machine. It is common for small machines to have three wheels, which increases the throat capacity without increasing the wheel size.

The wheels of the bandsaw are usually fitted with rubber tyres. These are crowned so that the speed of rotation causes the blade to climb to the highest point of the camber. The top wheel is normally adjustable for tensioning the blade and for tracking. Narrow blades, having less mass, require less tension than the wider blades. At the end of the day's work it is a good practice to reduce the tension on the blade. The tracking screw is a means of adjusting the tilt of the top pulley so that the blade follows the correct path as it moves.

The bandsaw has an adjustable saw guide which gives support to the back of the blade by a bronze thrust wheel and gives lateral support by the means of fibre pads. This saw guide is always adjusted so that it just clears the surface of the work, thereby giving maximum support to the blade.

This is generally considered to be a very safe machine to use. The rule is to tension the blade before starting the machine to check the tracking. Set the guide to just over the thickness of the work and keep the hands away from the right-hand side of the blade because if the blade should break it will generally fly out on that side. Keep the blade sharp and set.

MACHINE PLANER

These machines consist of a steel cylinder fitted with either two or three knife-like blades. The machine size is known by the length of the cutting cylinder and can be from about 4in (100mm) to 20in (510mm). Obviously the larger the machine the more power it consumes and the more expensive it is to run. The cutting cylinder normally revolves at about 6,000 revolutions per minute.

Mounted on either side of the cutting cylinder are two sturdy steel tables. These are adjustable in height and can be operated independently of each other. The method of adjustment is effected by moving each table along a ramp by means of adjusting screws. In this fashion it is possible to work to very fine limits. The machine tables are normally graduated in 1/16in (1.5mm) but there is every possibility of working to 1/64in (0.5mm).

In operation the back table is always set level with the tips of the cutters. This can be checked by switching the machine on and running a piece of previously planed wood from the back table onto the cutters. A snicking noise should be heard as the cutters just touch the wood.

The depth of cut is arranged by lowering the front table the desired amount below the back table. Most machine planers can deal with a thickness of cut up to $\frac{1}{2}$in (12mm) at one pass. It is wrong to attempt to cut less than 1/16in (1.5mm) as the cutters will only be rubbing and will quickly dull. Similarly it is wrong to attempt to machine plane timber of less than 8in (200mm) in length as the gap between the two tables where the cutting cylinder revolves is about 1$\frac{3}{8}$in (35mm) wide and it is easy for the fingers to be caught.

To help prevent accidents it is normal to have a bridge guard fitted to the machine. This must always be set so that the wood can just pass between the guard and the cutters, the hands having to pass over the top of the guard.

When working at this machine always place the wood hollow side down on the infeed table. Check the direction of the grain on the timber as the work can be reversed to keep tearing to a minimum. A machine planer always cuts a ripple finish. The best finish is obtained from the planer by slow feeding; the ripples are then closest together and less conspicuous. On first class work, however, even this fine finish can be improved by hand planing. Remember that a high gloss finish will always expose marks on the wood rather than conceal them.

If the machine planer works unsatisfactorily it may be that the back table is incorrectly set, or that the cutters are blunt. It is easier to sharpen this machine if the cutters are left in place. Turn the block so that one cutter is $\frac{1}{4}$in (6mm) forward of the top position and lock the block in place with a wedge. Wrap two-thirds of a fine oilstone (8in x 2in x 1in size) with paper and rest the covered part of the stone on the back table, with the exposed stone over the cutting blade. Lower the back table until by sliding the stone along it touches the blade. Sharpen the cutting edge. A little oil will help. Turn the block around and sharpen the other cutters in the same manner. The stone, having been run along the blade, will not raise a burr. Most cutters are made from high speed steel and require sharpening about every two days of continuous use. Eventually the cutters will require re-grinding, and for this they are sent away to specialists, who will also balance them to reduce vibration and increase safety.

The purpose of the machine planer is

1   To prepare sawn timber to a smooth finish.
2   To make the surfaces flat and out of wind, and square to each other.
3   To prepare the timber to an even thickness.

There are three types of planing machine. The simplest, the overhand or surfacer, is the one that has been described. This will make the surface smooth and flat and can prepare surfaces square to each other, but it will not thickness the material. This has to be done on a special machine called a thicknesser. These two machines can be bought combined in one, and they are then known as an over and under. Wood is surfaced over the top of the machine and thicknessed by passing back under the cutting block of the machine. The third type of machine, the four-cutter, will perform the whole planing procedure in one operation.

PORTABLE ELECTRIC ROUTER

The electric router is capable of performing many more tasks than the simple hand router. It is in effect an inverted spindle moulder and can be used to produce all manner of mouldings.

The electric router consists of a powerful motor (about 1 horsepower) which runs at a very fast speed (20,000-30,000 rpm). The motor fits into a housing which is fitted with two handles to help guide the tool. The whole tool weighs less than 10lb, is fairly quiet and easy to handle.

Cutting bits are fitted directly to the spindle of the motor by means of a collet type chuck. The motor is adjustable inside the housing so that the bit can be extended to a predetermined depth below the sole of the machine and the depth can be set to an accuracy of about 0.004in. In operation the fast spinning cutter of the machine cuts very cleanly. It will make easy work of a groove. The router is always fed from left to right. A fence is provided to follow the edge of the work. Alternatively a batten can be cramped down to the work and the edge of the machine allowed to follow the batten.

Many different shaped cutters are available in either high speed steel or tungsten carbide. The latter is very expensive but stays sharp for a long time. The cutters can groove and rebate, flute, round over edges, cove, chamfer and dovetail. Furthermore, the tool can make joints such as housings, dovetail housings, tongue and groove. The electric router will also trim Formica.

ELECTRIC DRILL

The electric drill consists of a fast revolving armature which is geared down to produce a chuck speed of about 3,000 revolutions per minute. Slower running drills of about 1,000 revolutions per minute are available for masonry drilling. Two-speed drills are also available and these offer considerable versatility. The size of the drill is known by the maximum diameter circular bar that the chuck can hold. This varies between $\frac{1}{4}$in (6mm) and $\frac{1}{2}$in (13mm).

The early electric drills were fitted with plain three jaw chucks, as fitted to the hand drill, but these have now been superseded by Jacobs geared chucks. A chuck key is used to tighten the grip of the chuck on the bit. Having closed the chuck jaws on the shank of the bit, the chuck key should be placed in one of the three spigot holes in the chuck body and normal pressure applied to the key. Check if further tightening is required, however slight, by applying the chuck key to the other spigot holes in turn.

Maintenance of the electric drill should be performed occasionally, according to instructions supplied with the tool. This will usually concern the carbon brushes which should not be less than 5/16in (8mm) in length and should always be replaced in pairs. The front gearbox will also require replenishing with grease. To do this the front section of the drill is removed by releasing two or three screws. Clean out the old grease with a stick. It is seldom advisable to wash out the gearbox with paraffin as this can thin the grease contained in the front bearing. Replenish with the correct grade of grease and do not exceed the original amount. When warm, grease expands and can cause loss of power and excessive overheating.

The electric drill can be given a long life by taking certain precautions. Do not clamp the drill in the vice as this will distort the frame. Coil the cables when not in use and keep them free of oil and grease. Do not lift the drill by the lead. Always keep the drill bits correctly sharpened and avoid switching the drill on under load. Switch on and run for a few seconds before drilling. This allows the drill to reach maximum speed. Do not apply excessive pressure as slowing the motor will cause overheating. If the machine becomes very hot allow to cool by running with no load for a few minutes before switching off.

Various attachments are available for most electric drills, chiefly sawing, sanding and grinding. Sawing is hard work for a drill so keep saw blades sharp. The electric drill is usually capable of sawing to a depth of 1½in (38mm). When bench sawing the drill is supported in a bench stand. Bolt the stand securely to your bench. The chuck of the drill will have to be removed by holding the spindle of the drill steady with the spanner provided whilst turning the chuck in the *same direction as it normally revolves,* using the chuck key as a lever. Some types of drill have no position for a spanner, in which case put the chuck key into one of the chuck spigot holes and tap the key with the handle of the hammer. The inertia of the gearing will oppose the force you apply.

A saw mandrel is screwed onto the drill in place of the chuck. The saw blade is then bolted to the mandrel with a metal washer either side of the blade for support. On some machines a spring saw guard is also bolted onto the mandrel with the blade. It is possible for the saw blade to be fitted backwards. A correctly fitted blade will have the points of the teeth of the saw coming over the top and towards the operator. Fit the table in position then check that the blade is free to revolve by rotating it by hand. Plug in the machine and start it up. Allow a short pause before cutting for the machine to reach maximum speed. Do not force wood through the saw or damage will occur to the motor. The machine cuts at its best when it is revolving at its fastest speed.

A useful sawing attachment is the jig saw. A short blade is moved rapidly up and down. This machine tool can be used for straight or contour sawing. Hold it so that the sole plate rests firmly on the work and feed along the line without forcing.

The disc sander as a bench machine is a handy accessory. A circular steel plate is attached to the spindle of the drill and to this steel disc is glued a circle of garnet paper. Usually the glue (disc cement) is in stick form and is applied to the disc as it rotates. Friction melts the glue. Stop the machine and press the sanding disc firmly in position. The finish obtained is quite good. Feed the work steadily without applying too much pressure as this would burn the wood. If a good thickness of material has to be removed feed the work through several times until the cut is completed. Generally a little hand sanding afterwards in the direction of the grain will further improve the finish.

The portable disc sander is a more difficult tool to operate successfully. A rubber backing pad is attached to the chuck of the drill and the sanding discs, supplied with a central hole, are bolted onto the pad with a recessed nut. The disc should not be placed flat on the work but held at an angle with only the trailing edge working. Allow the speed of the disc to do the work. Do not press as this will slow the motor and cause rings to appear on the work.

The finishing sander cuts slowly and gives a very smooth finish for painting or sanding. Rectangular sanding sheets are clipped across a rubber sole which either oscillates or moves in very small orbits. Do not press on the machine but pass it over the work as if ironing a sheet. This machine is not suitable for finishing a rough sawn surface but it will remove the ripple marks left on the surface by a machine planer.

Chapter 8

Basic Procedures

DESIGN

The process of design is composed of four steps.

1 Consider the function of the article. This will at the very least suggest the overall sizes and can give ideas on the layout and form. For an item to be truly successful it must work well.

2 Think about the construction. Consider how it is to be made, whether it can be put together easily and the size and strength of the various members.

3 Consider the proportion of the pieces. Perhaps a wider rail may make the article look more balanced, more aesthetically pleasing. A little shaping can alter the appearance and indeed make the item more functional.

4 Some carefully applied decoration can add appeal to the article. This could be achieved by the colourful effect of different timbers. Texture, too, can be thought about in the quality of finish that is to be used. Decoration can also be added by the use of chamfers, carving, or inlay.

The current fashion is for simply decorated designs, the main effect of the item being its shape and form. Whatever you think of this you must design things so that they are relevant to your needs. Use the opportunity to create things the way you wish, avoid using direct copy, and you will achieve greater satisfaction.

PREPARING A DRAWING

A sketch should be made at the beginning of any job. It can be invaluable both as an aid to memory and to prevent constructional mistakes. For those people who find drawing difficult it can take the form of a thumbnail sketch showing principally the overall dimensions.

Most designers begin by making many simple sketches, developing their ideas as they work. A small scale drawing always looks most realistic if it is drawn to a scale of $\frac{1}{8}$ or 1/10, as the view shown on paper in front of you looks approximately the same as the finished object standing at the normal viewing distance.

These scale drawings can be turned into models using either balsa wood or the wood that is to be used in the final construction. Balsa cement or PVA glue will hold the parts of the model together. A full-size model can always be made using cheap softwood (or cardboard) with parts roughly nailed together. People often say they can work well without making sketches or models by designing the job as they go. In point of fact they are trying to take a short cut and this can lead to mistakes that are impossible or expensive to rectify.

The final drawings can show greater detail if important parts are drawn full size. Many examples of such working drawings are included in chapter 9. Due to difficulties in reproduction these drawings may not show parts exactly full size.

MAKING A CUTTING LIST

Having prepared the drawings, the next stage is to make a cutting list. The timber merchant will not want to see the drawings but he will expect to be given a detailed analysis showing exactly the materials required.

The first essential is the type of timber required. Sometimes two or three timbers are used in the construction of an article and the parts needed should be separated under their respective headings, viz African mahogany, chipboard, plywood, etc.

The next requirement is the quantities of similar items, viz 4 legs, 2 side rails, 2 end rails.

Demensioning of the items requires care. The first dimension is always the length. This is taken in the direction of the grain and it may not be the greatest dimension of a piece of wood. In fact it is quite common for a piece of wood to be wider than it is long. Included in the length should be an extra $\frac{1}{2}$in (12mm). This will allow $\frac{1}{4}$in (6mm) at each end for sawing the ends square. The second dimension given is the width, and to this should be added $\frac{1}{4}$in (6mm) to allow for planing. This is then called the nominal size, though a better system is to ask for the finished size (f). This means planed and finished to this size, so 3in (nom) = $2\frac{3}{4}$in (f). The third dimension given is the thickness. To this can be added $\frac{1}{8}$ (3mm) for planing, although most times the finished size is the most convenient to use.

An example of a cutting list for four legs of a stool which must finish 16in (410mm) high, $1\frac{3}{8}$in (35mm) wide and $1\frac{1}{4}$in (32mm) thick, is:

4 legs teak $16\frac{1}{2}$in (422mm) f x $1\frac{3}{8}$in (35mm) f x $1\frac{1}{4}$in (32mm) f

ORDERING TIMBER

There are usually a variety of places in every town where one can buy timber, but it is not always appreciated that each firm specialises in certain woods and manufactured boards. The do-it-yourself (handyman) shop is always helpful but it specialises in softwood and manufactured board. Only a few of these shops stock hardwood. The advantage of a do-it-yourself shop is that it will usually cut to any size, and this can save time and money.

Many joinery and shopfitting firms can be very obliging, and they are well equipped with machinery and can supply your exact requirements. It should be realised that these people are manufacturers rather than suppliers so be prepared to wait two or three weeks for your order to be processed.

The large firms usually specialise in either hardwood or softwood. The softwood section of the timber trade is an entirely distinct division from the hardwood section; even the units of measurement are different. Hardwoods are bought by the cubic foot, whereas softwoods are bought by the standard. A standard of softwood is 165 cubic feet. This is now changing in the UK where the standard is being replaced by the cubic metre. Some large firms will not serve the customer with a small order, but others can be quite helpful. It is a question of finding the right firm.

Always try to order the timber planed on four surfaces as this will save you much time and effort. Make it clear to the

L

timber merchant that the sizes given are the finished measurements of the timber after machine planing, indicating this by the letter (f).

ORDER OF CONSTRUCTION

With all jobs there is an order of construction that can be followed. This will speed up work and make mistakes less likely. The procedure is as follows.

1   Set out the parts and number adjacent joints. Pencil the number on the *outside* surface. The reference marks will then remain on the work until after the job has been glued together. Mark the face sides and face edges if this will help.

2   Mark the pieces of wood to length. Knife lines should be used as these are guide lines for the saw. Do not saw the wood to length too early. If the first joint is not successful it may be that sufficient wood remains to cut another without reducing the dimensions of the article.

3   Mark out the joints.

4   Make sure all the necessary marking out is done before commencing to cut; then choose the most important joint and cut this first. Follow the advice of checking twice and cutting once! Do not remove the wrong part for waste. A sound idea is to hatch in the waste areas with a pencil before cutting.

5   Fit the joints using either a hammer and block of wood or a sash cramp to close the joint. Do not glue up yet.

6   When all the joints have been fitted take the pieces apart and clean up the inside surfaces with a smoothing plane. Remove just two shavings and keep the use of glasspaper to a minimum.

7   Polish the inside surfaces, as these will be inaccesible after glueing up. Wax the inside surfaces to prevent glue from sticking, but take care not to put wax on the joints, as this will reduce their strength.

8   Cramp up without glue and use waste wood to prevent the shoes of the cramps from marking the work. This will set the cramps to length. Check that the joints fit really well; check too for squareness and twist before proceeding.

GLUEING UP

Before glueing up check that the room is warm. Scotch glue gels too quickly in a cold room, and formaldehyde glues are slow to set. Mark where each joint goes as this will speed up work. Do not be over ambitious. It is better to glue up some of the work the next day rather than find the glue setting before you are finished.

Always glue both surfaces of the joint. Work quickly and wipe off excess glue with a damp rag before it hardens. Do not overtighten the cramps as this will distort the work.

Make careful tests before leaving the work to set.

1 Check the diagonals for equal length. This will ensure squareness. If incorrect try moving the cramps slightly in the direction of the long diagonal.

2 Sight for twist. This can be corrected by moving the cramps. or packing the end of one cramp off the bench with a piece of wood.

3 Check that the joints are closed and fit up tight.

Next day the cramps can be removed and the outside surfaces of the work cleaned up with a smoothing plane. Plane protruding parts of the joints flush and remove all pencil and knife lines. Round over any sharp corners on the work and this will add a professional touch making the item much nicer to handle. Polish the outside of the work to match the treatment given to the inside surfaces.

LAP BUTT JOINT (fig 93)

☐ MARKING OUT THE JOINT

Assuming that the wood has been planed to size and sawn to length, square up the ends on the shooting board.

A Arrange the parts and if necessary number them in pairs.
B Set a cutting gauge to just over the thickness of the wood.
C Use this setting to gauge the shoulder line across the inside surface and one-third way across the edge.
D Set a marking gauge to one-third thickness of the wood. Hold the wood in the vice and gauge across the end and

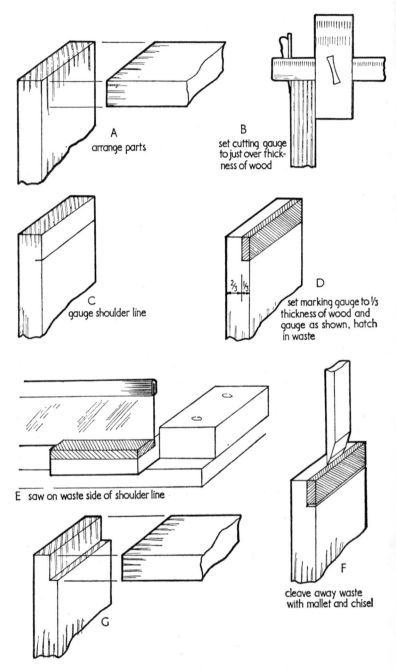

A
arrange parts

B
set cutting gauge
to just over thick-
ness of wood

C
gauge shoulder line

D
set marking gauge to ⅓
thickness of wood and
gauge as shown, hatch
in waste

⅔ ⅓

E saw on waste side of shoulder line

F
cleave away waste
with mallet and chisel

G

Fig 93 Lap butt joint. Marking out and cutting this joint

down to the shoulder line. Hatch in the waste with a
pencil.

☐ CUTTING THE JOINT
  E Place the work on a bench hook and saw along the waste
     side of the shoulder line with a tenon saw.
  F Stand the wood upright in the vice and with an inch
     (25mm) chisel and mallet, cleave away the waste in stages.
     Alternatively the waste may be removed with a tenon saw
     as when sawing a tenon (see later in this chapter).

THROUGH DOVETAIL JOINT (figs 94 & 95)

☐ MARKING OUT THE TAILS
  A Number the joints on the outside surfaces, then mark the
     shoulder lines the thickness of the wood plus 1/16in
     (1.5mm) in from the ends using a marking knife and try
     square. If the ends are square a cutting gauge may be
     used as an alternative.
  B Mark out the position of the tails in pencil on the
     shoulder line of one of the pieces.
  C Use a dovetail template to complete the marking out. A
     slope of 1 in 6 is used for softwoods and 1 in 8 for hard-
     woods. Hatch in the waste.

☐ CUTTING THE TAILS
  D & E Place the wood for the tails low in the vice to pre-
     vent undue vibration when sawing. Slope the work so
     that the lines are vertical and with a dovetail saw cut
     down *on the lines* to the shoulder line.
  F The waste on the outsides may be removed by placing
     the wood horizontally in the vice and cutting on the
     waste side of the line with a dovetail saw.
  G & H The coping saw may be used to remove most of the
     waste between the tails. The remainder can be chiselled
     back to the shoulder line with a bevelled edge chisel. It
     is a good policy to work on a chiselling board using a
     straight piece of wood cramped along the shoulder line
     as a guide.

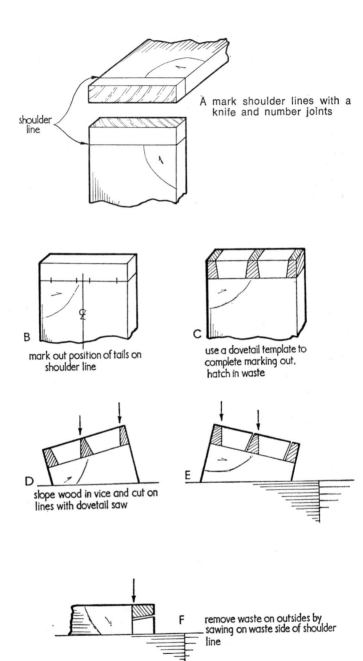

A mark shoulder lines with a knife and number joints

shoulder line

B mark out position of tails on shoulder line

C use a dovetail template to complete marking out, hatch in waste

D slope wood in vice and cut on lines with dovetail saw

E

F remove waste on outsides by sawing on waste side of shoulder line

Figs 94 & 95 Through dovetail joint

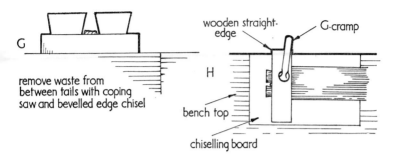

G

remove waste from
between tails with coping
saw and bevelled edge chisel

H

wooden straight-
edge

G·cramp

bench top

chiselling board

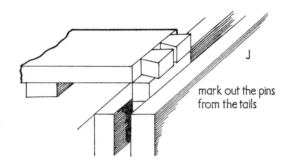

J

mark out the pins
from the tails

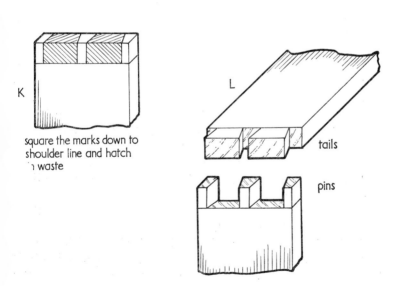

K

square the marks down to
shoulder line and hatch
ｎ waste

L

tails

pins

☐ MARKING OUT THE PINS

J Place number 1 piece for the pins in the vice and arrange
the tails for number 1 across it. Check for squareness
with a try square and ensure that the tails are positioned
correctly over the wood for the pins. Mark around the
tails with a scriber. This can be a piece of broken hack-
saw blade sharpened to a point or the blade of a small
penknife. Sometimes it is difficult to see the scriber
marks, in which case the end grain of the pins can be
rubbed with chalk before marking.

K Square the marks down the sides of the wood to the
shoulder line with a pencil. Hatch in the waste.

☐ CUTTING THE PINS

When cutting the pins there is no need to slope the wood
in the vice. Cut down on the *waste side of the lines* with the
dovetail saw and remove most of the waste with a coping saw.
The waste that remains may be carefully pared away with the
bevelled edge chisel in a similar manner to that used when
cutting the tails. It is easiest to work from each side into the
centre of the wood.

STUB MORTISE AND TENON JOINT (figs 96 & 97)

☐ MARKING OUT THE JOINT

Assuming the wood has been planed to size and sawn to
length

B   Place the piece in which the mortise is to be cut in the
vice and rest the other piece across it. Check the position of
the top piece with a steel rule and try square.

C   Mark against both edges of the top piece with a pencil
and square these marks across the upper surface. These lines
are the shoulder lines for the joint.

D   If several similar joints are to be cut mark all shoulder
lines together with a pencil.

E   Mark $\frac{1}{8}$in (3mm) *inside* the shoulder lines with a pencil
and square these marks across. These are the mortise-limit
lines and will allow a cover on the tenon to conceal the
mortise.

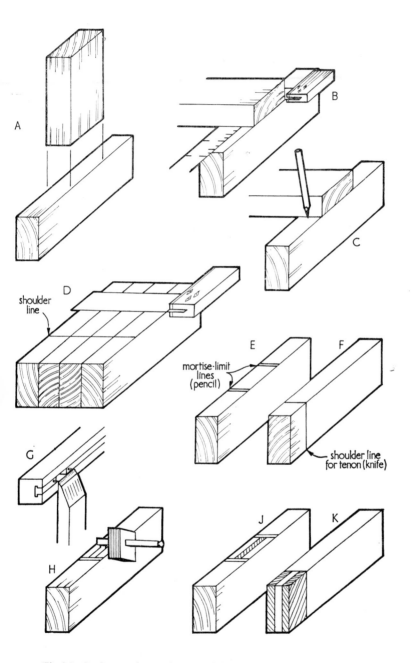

Fig 96 Stub mortise and tenon joint. Marking out the joint

F   Mark the shoulder line for the tenon with a marking knife and square the line all the way round. The length of a stub tenon is usually two-thirds the width of the wood.

G   Set a mortise chisel nearest one-third the thickness of the wood, then check the marks made from both edges to make the joint central.

H   Gauge the mortise and the tenon from the face side.

J & K   Hatch in the waste with a pencil.

☐ CUTTING THE MORTISE

L   G cramp the wood to the end of the bench.

M   With the flat part of the chisel facing towards oneself make two cuts and remove the wood from the notch.

N   Using a mallet, work away from the notch. Mark the depth of the mortise on the chisel with chalk or coloured tape to prevent cutting too deep. Several passes will have to be made to enable the chisel to reach full depth.

O   To remove the waste put the wood in the vice and carefully lever out the chips. Do not use a mallet and take care not to round the corners.

P   Hold the wood upright in the vice. Place the tenon saw just outside the gauge line and saw a shallow groove.

Q   Slope the wood in the vice to 45° and saw down to the diagonals.

R   Hold the wood upright in the vice and cut straight down to the shoulder line.

S   Place the work on a bench hook and, keeping on the waste side of the shoulder line, remove the cheeks taking care not to cut into the tenon.

T   Finally mark $\frac{1}{8}$in (3mm) and remove waste at ends of tenon for covers.

DOWEL JOINTS (fig 99)

☐ METHODS OF LOCATING THE DOWEL

A   A manufactured jig (fig 98). This will require a centre line to be marked for the joint in pencil.

B   A home-made jig. This will only work on a flat frame with all pieces the same thickness.

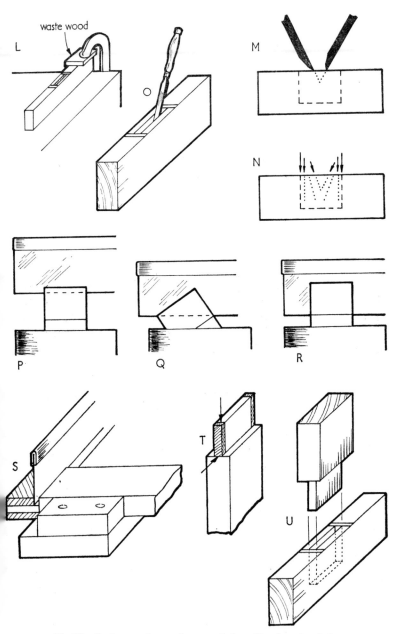

Fig 97 Stub mortise and tenon joint. Cutting the joint

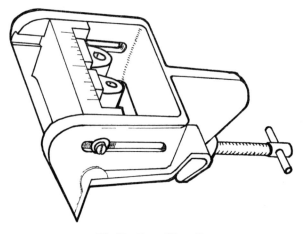

Fig 98 Dowelling jig

C Panel pins. The panel pins should be driven part way in one piece and the heads cut off just above the surface of the wood. Align the two pieces and tap both together. This transfers the dowel positions onto the other piece. Remove pins with pincers before drilling.

☐ MAKING DOWEL

D Square straight-grained stuff should be prepared which is cleft, ie cut with a chisel or axe. Point one end and hammer the piece through a dowel plate. This is a steel plate drilled with a series of holes, $\frac{5}{8}$in, $\frac{1}{2}$in, $\frac{3}{8}$in, (16mm, 13mm, 10mm). Place the dowel plate over a hole in the bench, eg remove the bench stop.

Dowel may be bought in lengths up to about 7ft (2m). Thickness of dowel varies from $\frac{1}{8}$in (3mm) to about 1in (25mm).

☐ FITTING DOWEL

Cut dowel to lengths just shorter than that required to fill the holes. This will prevent the dowels resting on the bottom of both holes thereby preventing the joint from closing.

A tight dowel should be eased before glueing to prevent glue from bursting open the wood.

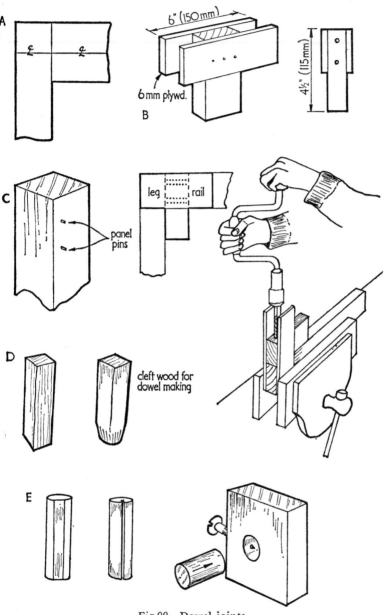

A

B

6" (150 mm)

6 mm plywd.

4½" (115 mm)

C

panel pins

leg   rail

D

cleft wood for dowel making

E

Fig 99   Dowel joints

E   To provide for glue escape the dowel may be either planed with a flat or it may be grooved. The groove method can be simply achieved. A block of wood is drilled with a drill the size of the dowel. A screw is inserted through the edge of the block until the point emerges in the hole. The dowel rod may be tapped through the hole and the dowel will be grooved as it emerges.

Chapter 9

Designs in Wood

WOODWORK BENCH

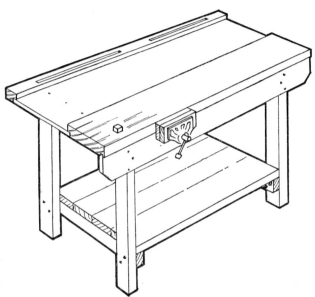

Fig 100   Woodwork bench. Pictorial view

This bench has been designed for the person who has a workshop or spare room large enough to contain a bench but with limited tools to hand. It can be built without the aid of another bench; the frame of the bench may be used to aid the work while the rest is being completed. The bench can easily be taken apart and put together again when moving house.

Despite its ease of construction this bench is most substantial. It has a solid hardwearing top of $1\frac{3}{4}$in (45mm) thick beech which is suitable for supporting work even when heavy morticing is being done by hand. Large section legs provide plenty of support for the top which has a 4in (100mm) overhang at each end to facilitate the use of G cramps. A wide

apron at the front and a diagonal brace at the back of the
bench top so it is not transmitted to other parts of the build-
saw movement when planing. Rubber feet let into the legs
help to isolate the noise made by machinery being used on the
bench make the whole construction rigid and prevent a seeing by the floorboards.

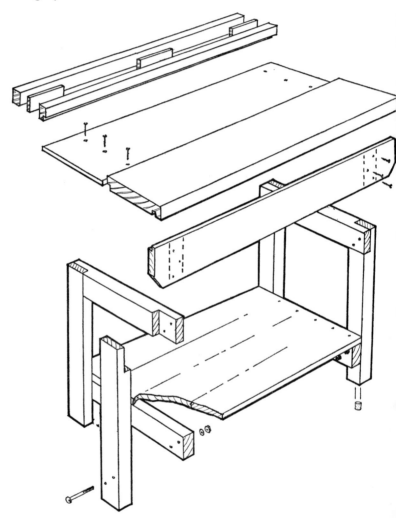

Fig 101   Woodwork bench. Exploded view with brace omitted

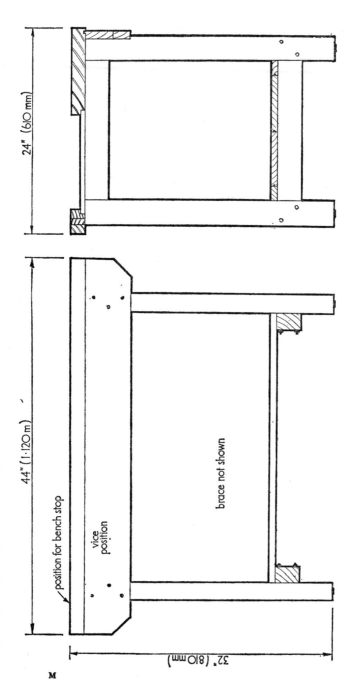

Fig 102 Woodwork bench. Working drawing

24" (610 mm)

44" (1·120 m)

32" (810 mm)

position for bench stop

vice position

brace not shown

M

It is advisable to check overall sizes and make alterations if required. The cutting list shows that the underframe is softwood, the well is plywood, and the top is beech. This top will be hard to work but this is unavoidable as a hardwearing top is required. Ask the timber merchant to cut the groove and rebates for you when ordering the timber (fig 103) as this will be a simple task for him on the machine planer and circular saw.

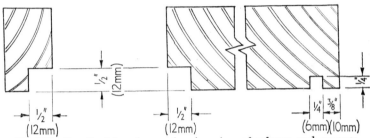

Fig 103   Detail of bench top showing sizes of rebates and grooves

☐   CUTTING LIST

Softwood

Legs	4	31in	3in	2in
		(790mm)	(75mm)	(50mm)
End rails	4	23in	3in	2in
		(580mm)	(75mm)	(50mm)
Apron	1	45in	6in	1in
		(1.140m)	(150mm)	(25mm)
Shelving	4	33in	6in	1in
		(840mm)	(150mm)	(25mm)
Brace	1	44in	3in	1in
		(1.120m)	(75mm)	(25mm)

Birch Plywood

Well	1	44in (f)	12in (f)	12in
		(1.120m)	(305mm)	(12mm)

Beech

Top	1	44in (f)	10in (f)	$1\frac{3}{4}$in (f)
		(1.120m)	(250mm)	(45mm)
Tool rack	2	44in (f)	1in (f)	$1\frac{3}{4}$in (f)
		(1.120m)	(25mm)	(45mm)
Tool rack	3	6in (f)	$\frac{3}{4}$in (f)	$1\frac{3}{4}$in (f)
		(150mm)	(20mm)	(45mm)

Hardware	8	4in x $\frac{1}{4}$in (100mm x 6mm) coach bolts with nut and washer
	4	rubber door stops for feet, about 1in (25mm) diameter

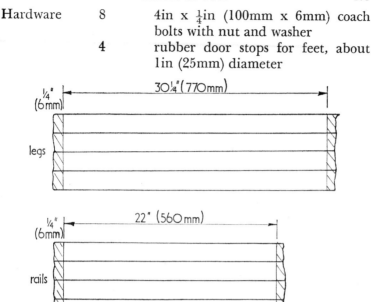

Fig 104   Marking rails and legs to length for woodwork bench

Mark out the legs and rails to length as shown in figure 104. Mark the pieces together as a set using a marking knife, try square, and steel rule, then separate the pieces and square the lines around each. Saw accurately to length with a tenon saw.

Mark out the position of the joints (fig 105) in pencil. W refers to the exact width of the timber and will of course be in the region of $2\frac{3}{4}$in (70mm).

Set a marking guage to half the thickness of the wood and gauge the corner halving. Mark the shoulder line with a marking knife working against a try square. Cut the corner halving joint either as you would a lap butt joint or a one-sided (barefaced) tenon. Screw and glue the corner halvings together.

Place the bottom rail in position and cramp firmly to the leg. Drill through the leg and rail. Bolt the rail in position with two coach bolts at each point.

Notch the apron around the legs by carefully marking the position then sawing across the grain and removing the waste with either a chisel or router to $\frac{1}{4}$in (6mm) depth.

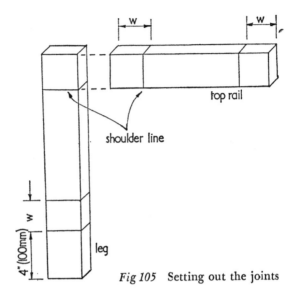

Fig 105 Setting out the joints

Prepare a tongue on the apron to fit the groove in the bench top. Use a rebate plane for this. Make sure that the correct part of the apron is removed—check twice and cut once! The tongue and groove may be glued together.

Make the rack for small tools by glueing the pieces together. Cramp until the glue has set.

Screw the apron front to the end frames. Leave this as a dry joint (do not glue); then the bench can be dismantled. The top can be fastened to the rails by metal brackets. Screw the plywood well to the rails and attach the tool rack with metal angle brackets. The shelf boards may be screwed to the lower end rails. Drill into the bottoms of the legs to take the rubber feet.

Figure 106 shows how the vice is fixed to the bench. A hole has to be cut in the apron front to allow part of the vice to pass through. Four $\frac{3}{8}$in (9mm) coach screws hold the vice securely in place under the bench top. Coach screws are merely wood screws that have a square head, these being turned with a box spanner. A clearance and pilot hole must be drilled to enable the screw to be tightened with reasonable ease. In most instances a packing piece has to be inserted between the vice

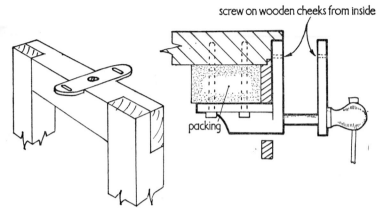

screw on wooden cheeks from inside

packing

Fig 106 Fixing of bench top to rails with metal plates. The elongated screw holes allow the top to expand and contract across the width

and underside of the top so that the top of the jaws may be ½in (12mm) below the surface of the bench. This is necessary to keep the teeth of the tenon saw away from the steel jaws of the vice. In this way accidential damage to the saw is prevented. A small rebate will have to be worked in the edge of the top with a chisel.

Two pieces of wood 10in (250mm) x 3½in (90mm) x ⅝in (15mm) must be fitted to the jaws of the vice. These will prevent bruising of the work. Two threaded holes are provided in each vice jaw to take 5/16in Whitworth set screws. These will hold the wooden cheeks in place.

PAINTED CABINET

☐ CUTTING LIST

Softwood

Top	1	23¾in	x	5¾in (f)	x	⅞in (f)	
		(600mm)		(145mm)		(22mm)	
Bottom	1	23¾in	x	5¾in (f)	x	⅝in (f)	
		(600mm)		(145mm)		(15mm)	
Sides	2	12¾in	x	5¾in (f)	x	⅝in (f)	
		(325mm)		(145mm)		(15mm)	

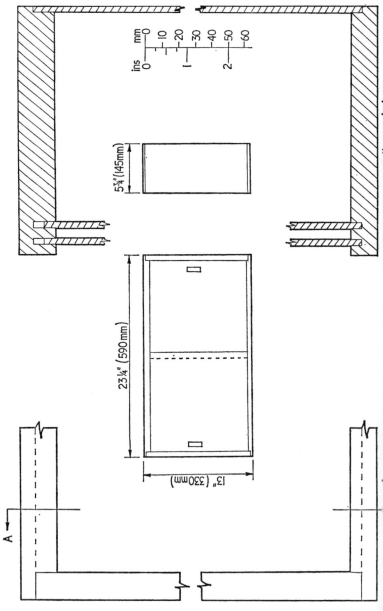

Fig 107 Painted cabinet. Working drawing

Shelf	1	22½in (570mm)	x	4in (f) (145mm)	x	⅜in (f) (10mm)
Hardboard						
Back & Doors	2	24in (610mm)	x	13in (330mm)	x	⅛in (3mm)

Choose the face side and face edge of each piece and mark with a pencil. These will be the outside surfaces.

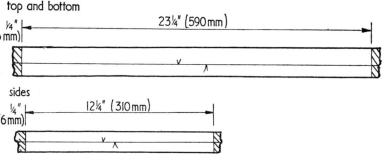

Fig 108   Painted cabinet. Marking to length

Mark out to length.

Mark out and cut a lap butt joint on top and bottom pieces to leave a ⅜in (9mm) tongue.

Plough grooves ⅛in (3mm) wide in top and bottom to contain the hardboard doors. Note that the groove in the top has to be twice the depth of the groove in the bottom. This is to enable the doors to be fitted after glueing up.

Rebate the bottom and sides ¼in (6mm) x ⅛in (3mm) for the hardboard back, and the top ½in (12mm) x ⅛in (3mm).

Clean up the inside surfaces. Pin and glue the joints together. Fit the back with number 16 gauge panel pins before cleaning up the outside and painting. Complete by fitting the doors with a 1¼in (30mm) overlap at the centre.

TRINKET BOX (Plate 2)

The box is made as a hollow block, then a saw cut is made all the way round to remove part for a lid. In this way the lid always fits the bottom of the box.

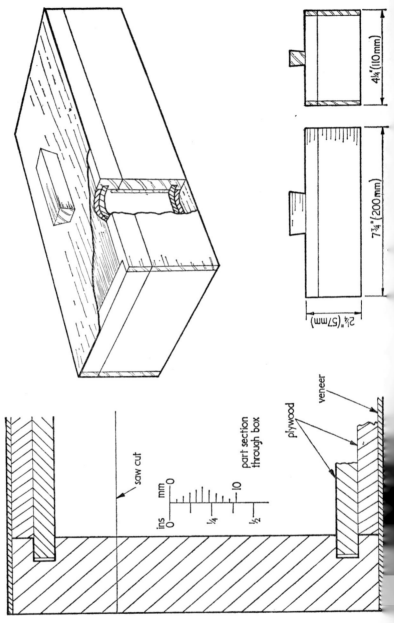

4¼" (110mm)

7¾" (200mm)

2¼" (57mm)

saw cut

part section
through box

mm
0

ins
0

¼

10

½

veneer

plywood

Fig 109   Trinket box. Working drawing

☐ CUTTING LIST

It is advisable to cut the sides and ends together so that the grooves may be made more easily.

Top & bottom	4	12¼in (310mm)	x	2⅜in (f) (60mm)	x	7/16in (f) (11mm)
Sides & ends	2	7¾in (200mm)	x	3¼in (f) (110mm)	x	3mm ply
Veneer	2	8in (210mm)	x	4½in (120mm)		
Lining	2	12in (310mm)	x	1½in (f) (40mm)	x	¼in (f) (6mm)
Handle	1	2½in (65mm)	x	¾in (f) (19mm)	x	¾in (f) (11mm)

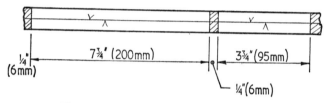

Fig 110 Trinket box. Marking to length

Mark out to length but do not cut until after the grooves have been worked. Support the wood in a sash cramp and hold the sash cramp in a vice when ploughing the grooves.

Cut the lap butt joint in the side pieces in the normal way. Clean up and polish the inside surfaces. Fit the box together and measure for the plywood top and bottom. Plane the plywood to size, then clean up with glasspaper and polish the inside surface.

Check that the box will go together, then glue up the main joints including the plywood top and bottom in the assembly.

When the glue has set fill in the well in the top and bottom with the other pieces of plywood. Glue these in place.

Now sand off the top and bottom surfaces *flat* on a disc sander. Alternatively a smoothing plane can be used to level these surfaces.

There are several methods of veneering but caul veneering is favoured in this instance. Spread an even layer of PVA glue

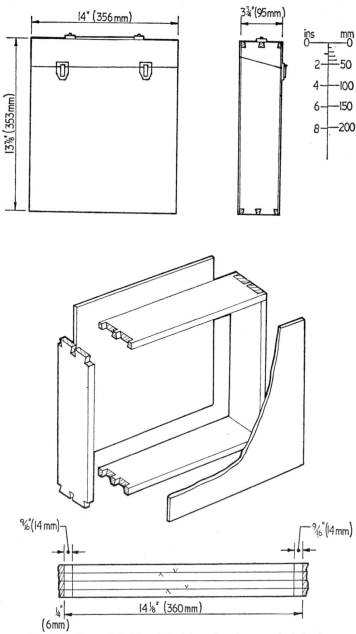

Fig 111 Record holder. Working drawing, exploded view and marking to length

to the top and bottom of the box taking particular care to glue up to the edges. Lay the veneer on the glued surface, then a blanket of paper, followed by a stout piece of plywood or blockboard. The latter is the caul and must be pressed down on the veneer with G cramps.

Carefully trim the overhanging veneer with a sharp knife. Glasspaper up the whole.

Mark a pencil line on the box for the lid position and separate either with a fine-toothed back saw or on a circular saw with the blade set low. Clean up the raw edge on the disc sander or by hand.

Polish the outside of the box and fit the lining by cutting a mitre on the corners.

A knob for the lid may be shaped with a plane, polished, and secured by two screws from the underside of the lid.

RECORD HOLDER

☐ CUTTING LIST

Hardwood	4	14¾in	x	3½in (f)	x	½in (f)
		(370mm)		(90mm)		(12mm)
Birch						
Plywood	2	14½in	x	14½in	x	4mm
		(370mm)		(370mm)		

Place the wood face edge upwards in the vice and mark to length (fig 111). Hatch in the waste with a pencil then mark in the shoulder line for the joint with a knife. Remove the wood from the vice and square the lines around each piece.

Saw off the waste and number the neighbouring joints on the outside surface (fig 112). Try to arrange the pieces with the grain matching on the corners.

Mark out the dovetails and cut in the normal way for a thorough dovetail joint. Fit the joints carefully. Tap them together with a hammer and block of wood. When correct, clean up and polish the inside surfaces.

Cramp up dry, then glue up. Check the diagonals for equal length. When the glue has set clean up the edges with a smoothing plane.

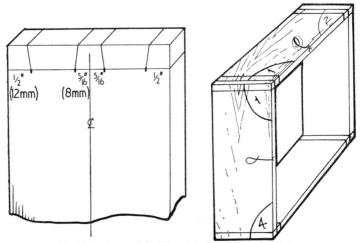

Fig 112 Record holder. Marking out the joints

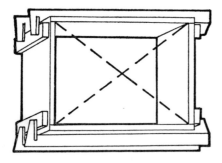

Fig 113 Record **holder.** Cramping up the frame and checking the diagonals for equal length

Fit the plywood to front and back. Secure in place with $\frac{3}{4}$in (19mm) No 4 chromium plated raised head screws. Avoid putting screws where they will interfere with sawing off the lid.

Mark a line for the lid position and cut through the box with a fine toothed back saw. Plane $\frac{1}{8}$in (3mm) from the plywood back to create a gap at the hinge position. Glue a 2in (50mm) wide strip of linen on either side of the plywood with contact adhesive. This forms a cloth hinge which is simple and unobtrusive, yet very strong. Cover the outside of the plywood with sticky-back plastic and allow some to wrap around the edges onto the inside. Cover the inside surface of the plywood

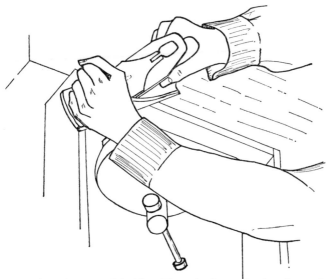

Fig 114 Record holder. Place the frame in the vice and clean
up the edges with a smoothing plane

with another piece of plastic and screw back onto the box. Fit
the handle with round-head screws and the catches with bi-
furcated rivets.

FLOWER TROUGH (Plate 3)

☐ CUTTING LIST

Trough	1	36in (915mm)	x	5in (130mm)	x	$\frac{5}{8}$in (f) (16mm)	
	2	7in (180mm)	x	8in (200mm)	x	$\frac{5}{8}$in (f) (16mm)	
	2	36in (915mm)	x	1in (f) (25mm)	x	$\frac{3}{8}$in (f) (10mm)	
	2	36in (915mm)	x	1$\frac{3}{16}$in (f) (30mm)	x	$\frac{3}{8}$in (f) (10mm)	
	2	36in (915mm)	x	1$\frac{3}{7}$in (f) (35mm)	x	$\frac{3}{8}$in (f) (10mm)	
Legs	4	32in (810mm)	x	2in (50mm)	x	1in (25mm)	

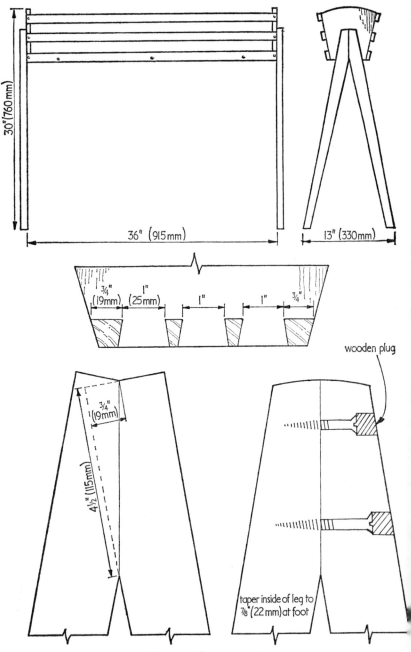

30" (760 mm)

36" (915 mm)

13" (330 mm)

¾" (19mm) 1" (25mm) 1" 1" ¾"

¾" (19mm)

4½" (115mm)

wooden plug

taper inside of leg to ⅞" (22 mm) at foot

Fig 115 Flower trough

The main strength of the flower trough is given by the two sets of through dovetail joints. When the legs are fitted these joints are concealed. The legs may be either screwed together, as illustrated, or dowel jointed.

This trough fits well in the alcove of a french window. Alternatively the legs can be replaced by feet and the trough stood on the window-sill. A plastic tray will catch drips from the flower pots.

COFFEE TABLE (Plate 4)

This is a coffee table of traditional design. The original was made entirely from solid mahogany.

To overcome the problem of continual expansion and contraction, the top is fastened to the frame with wooden buttons. The construction of buttons is explained later. Notice how the underside of the top has been chamfered to give a thinner, more delicate appearance to the edge of the table top. The legs are not square in section. The wider surface is placed on the side frame to balance the proportions.

☐ CUTTING LIST

Legs	4	18in	x	$1\frac{3}{8}$in (f) x	$1\frac{1}{4}$in (f)
		(460mm)		(35mm)	(32mm)
Rails	2	30in	x	$2\frac{3}{4}$in (f) x	$\frac{3}{4}$in (f)
		(760mm)		(70mm)	(19mm)
	2	14in	x	$2\frac{3}{4}$in (f) x	$\frac{3}{4}$in (f)
		(360mm)		(70mm)	(19mm)
Top	1	33in	x	$16\frac{1}{2}$in (f) x	$\frac{5}{8}$in (f)
		(840mm)		(420mm)	(16mm)

The top may have to be several pieces which are edge jointed together.

Make a face side mark on the best $1\frac{3}{8}$in surface of the leg, then make a face edge mark on the best edge. These reference sides will be on the outside of the finished job.

Mark the legs to length and hatch in the waste. Mark the mortise limit lines with a pencil. Square the knife lines all the way round each leg but square the pencil lines only onto

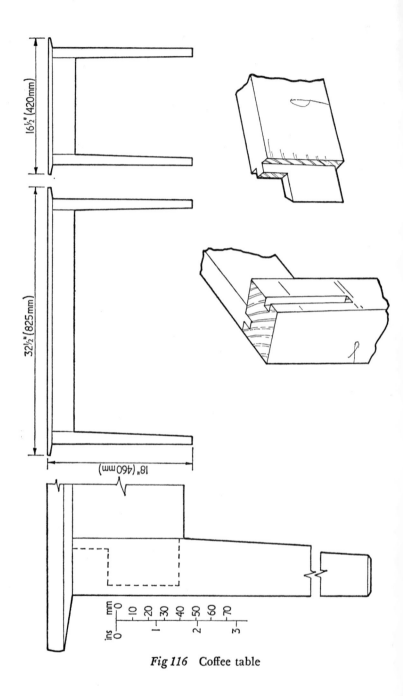

16½" (420mm)

32½" (825mm)

18" (460mm)

mm 0 10 20 30 40 50 60 70
ins 0 1 2 3

Fig 116 Coffee table

the other inside surface. Mark the rails to length and mark in the shoulder lines. Saw the rails to length.

Set the spurs of a mortise gauge to $\frac{1}{4}$in (6mm) mortise chisel. Set the stock of the gauge $\frac{1}{4}$in from the adjustable spur in order to mark in the centre on the edge of the rail. Gauge the mortises and tenons the normal way working from the face side in each case.

Cut the mortise proper. That is to say leave the haunch alone. The mortises will meet inside the leg. Saw the tenon in the normal way. The tenon has now to be cut down to size. Mark $\frac{1}{8}$in (3mm) cover at the bottom in pencil. The tenon will occupy two-thirds the width of the rail. The haunch is like a shorter tenon, being $\frac{1}{4}$in (6mm) long. Mark the haunch in pencil and remove the waste with a tenon saw. Saw down the sides of the mortise to $\frac{1}{4}$in deep and chisel out the waste to form the haunch in the leg. Mitre the ends of the tenons to prevent fouling in the mortise.

When the joints fit correctly, number them and clean up and polish the inside surfaces. Cramp up the two big frames dry. Check each framework carefully and when correct glue the two large frames separately. *On no account attempt to glue the whole table together in one stage.* When the glue has set cramp the whole up dry. Check carefully and when correct glue up.

Clean up all the outside surfaces. Do not leave sharp corners (arrises). Round corners to about $\frac{1}{8}$in radius circle using a smoothing plane or glasspaper. Polish when ready.

The top can be prepared as for a normal piece of timber. Should it be made up from several pieces, place pairs of boards together in the vice and plane the adjacent edges flat and square. Glue the edges and cramp the boards together (see sash cramp). The edges of the top should be carefully rounded. Glasspaper the end grain to make it smooth. When well pleased with the surface, it can be polished.

Table tops can be secured to the rails with metal angle plates but the traditional method of holding the top in place is with wooden buttons (fig 117). For this a mortise is chopped $1\frac{1}{4}$in (32mm) long with a $\frac{1}{4}$in (6mm) mortise chisel. The mortise is positioned $\frac{1}{2}$in (12mm) from the top edge of the rail.

The buttons for one table can be constructed together. For

N

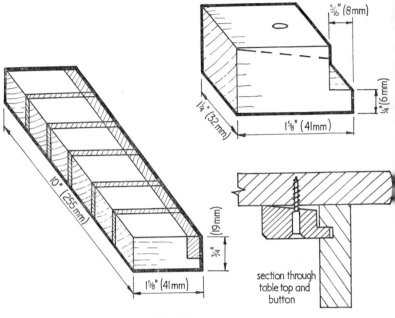

Fig 117   Buttons

six buttons select a sound piece of hardwood finished to 1⅝in
(41mm) x 10in (260mm) x ¾in (19mm). Note the direction of
the grain.

Mark each individual button 1¼in (32mm) wide and leave
¼in (6mm) space for waste between each. Now draw the diagonals on each button. This will give the position for the screw.
Rebate the edge to leave a 5/16in x ¼in tongue (fig 117) and drill
3/16in for the screws. Countersink for a No 8 screw and plane
the strip to finish as shown in the sectional diagram. Finally
saw the buttons from the strip and polish them.

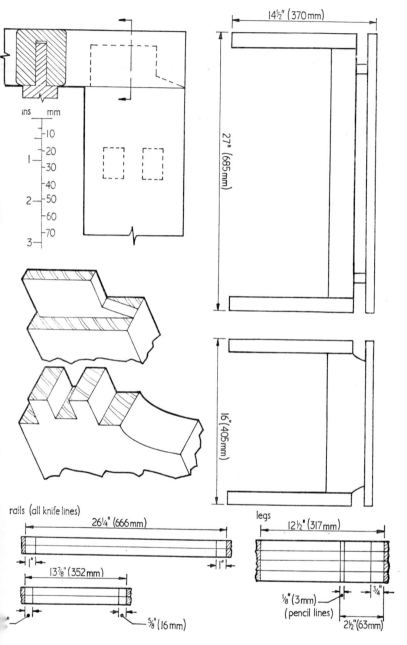

ins   mm

-10
-20
1 -30
-40
2 -50
-60
-70
3

14½" (370mm)

27" (685mm)

16" (405mm)

rails (all knife lines)

26¼" (666mm)

1"   1"

13⅞" (352mm)

⅝" (16mm)

legs

12½" (317mm)

⅛" (3mm)
(pencil lines)

¾"

2½"(63mm)

Fig 118 Table with floating top

TABLE WITH FLOATING TOP (Plate 5)

☐ CUTTING LIST

Legs	4	13in (330mm)	x	$1\frac{3}{8}$in (f) x (35mm)	$7\frac{1}{4}$in (f) (32mm)
Rails	2	27in (700mm)	x	$2\frac{1}{2}$in (f) x (63mm)	$\frac{7}{8}$in (f) (22mm)
	2	16in (400mm)	x	$3\frac{3}{4}$in (f) x (95mm)	$\frac{7}{8}$in (f) (22mm)
Top (blockboard)					
	1	27in (f) x (685mm)		16in (f) x (410mm)	$\frac{3}{4}$in (f) (19mm)

Fix the top by screwing up through the cross rails.

TEA TROLLEY (Plate 6)

☐ CUTTING LIST

Hardwood	4	$26\frac{1}{2}$in (680mm)	x	$1\frac{1}{4}$in (f) x (32mm)	$1\frac{1}{4}$in (f) (32mm)
	4	30in (760mm)	x	3in (f) x (76mm)	$\frac{3}{4}$in (f) (19mm)
	4	18in (460mm)	x	3in (f) x (76mm)	$\frac{3}{4}$in (f) (19mm)
Plywood shelves					
	2	30in (760mm)	x	18in (460mm)	x	4mm

Two battens glued across the underside of each shelf will give increased rigidity.

SMALL UPHOLSTERED STOOL (Plate 8)

☐ CUTTING LIST

Legs	4	$16\frac{1}{2}$in (420mm)	x	$2\frac{1}{4}$in (f) x (57mm)	$\frac{7}{8}$in (f) (22mm)
Top end rails	2	$9\frac{1}{2}$in (240mm)	x	$2\frac{1}{4}$in (f) x (63mm)	$\frac{7}{8}$in (f) (22mm)
Lower end rails	2	$9\frac{1}{2}$in (240mm)	x	$2\frac{1}{4}$in (f) x (57mm)	$\frac{7}{8}$in (f) (22mm)
Cross rails	3	$15\frac{1}{2}$in (400mm)	x	$2\frac{1}{4}$in (f) x (57mm)	$\frac{3}{8}$in (f) (22mm)

Materials for the seat are also required.

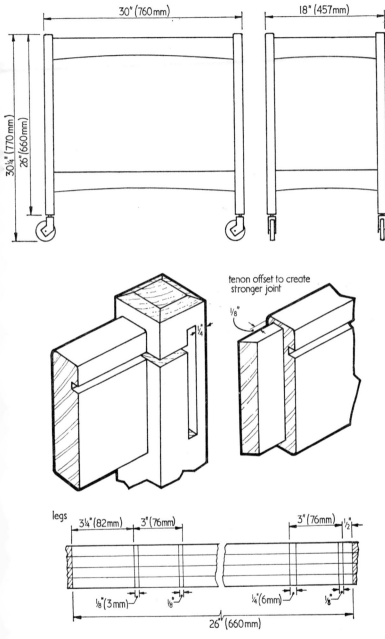

30" (760 mm)   18" (457mm)

30¼" (770 mm)
26" (660 mm)

tenon offset to create
stronger joint

¼"

⅛"

legs

3¼" (82mm)   3" (76mm)   3" (76mm)   ½"

⅛" (3 mm)   ⅛"   ¼" (6mm)   ⅛"

26" (660mm)

Fig 119   **Tea trolley**

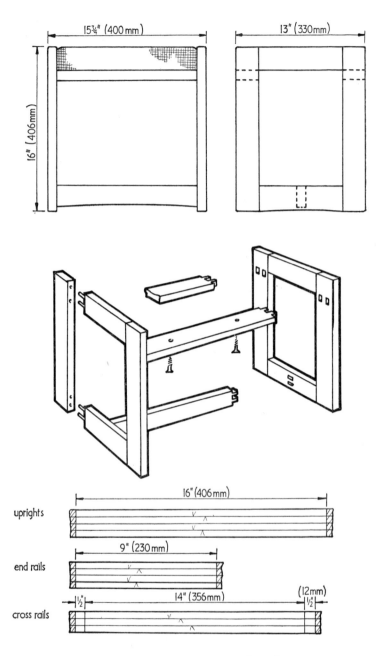

Fig 120 Small upholstered stool

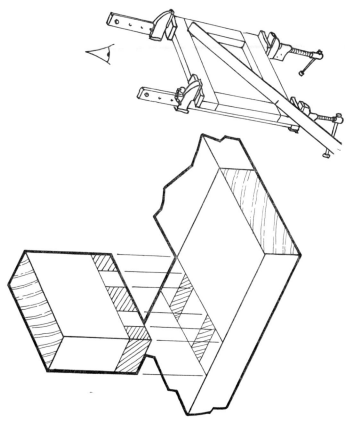

Fig 121 Small upholstered stool. Checking framework for squareness
and flatness. Marking out the joint

Work on the side frames first. Dowel the joints together,
clean up and polish the inside edges, then glue up. Take care
that the frames are identical in shape and size. Sight across
each frame for twist, check the diagonals for equal length, and
correct any discrepancy that is discovered before leaving the
frames for the glue to set. Mark out and cut the joints for the
cross rails after the side frames have been glued up.

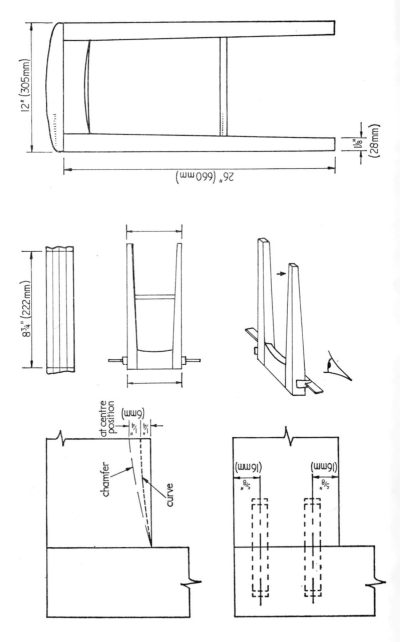

Fig 122   High stool

HIGH STOOL (Plate 7)

Legs	4	$26\frac{1}{2}$in	x	$1\frac{5}{8}$in (f) x	$1\frac{5}{8}$in (f)
		(680mm)		(41mm)	(41mm)
Rails	4	$9\frac{1}{4}$in	x	$2\frac{1}{2}$in (f) x	$\frac{7}{8}$in (f)
		(240mm)		(63mm)	(22mm)

Kicking Rails of aluminium or stainless steel.

4ft   x $\frac{5}{8}$in diameter

1.200m   16mm

The legs are drilled for these and *araldite* will secure them in place.

This is a more difficult model to assemble than the small stool so take special care when checking for truth.

Material is required for the seat.

☐ UPHOLSTERING THE TOP

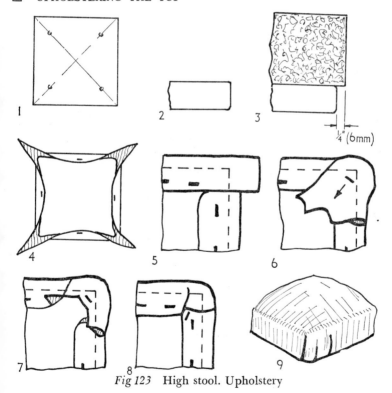

Fig 123 High stool. Upholstery

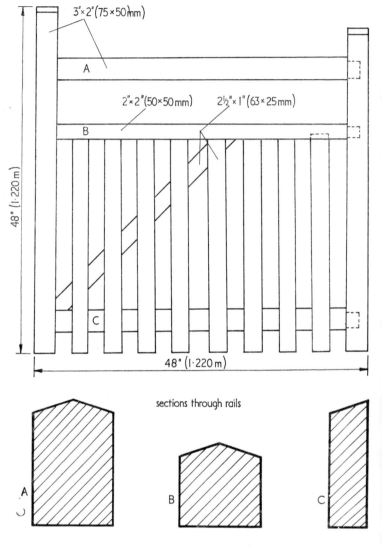

3″×2″(75×50 mm)

A

2″×2″(50×50 mm)   2½″×1″(63×25 mm)

B

48″ (1·220 m)

C

48″ (1·220 m)

sections through rails

A

B

C

Fig 124 **Garden gate**

Covering: vinyl leathercloth with flexknit backing.

1 Cut the seat to size in $\frac{1}{2}$in plywood or $\frac{3}{4}$in blockboard. Drill four air escape holes.

2 Round off the sharp edges with a rasp or plane. This will prevent the top covering being cut through in use.

3 The 2in foam should be cut $\frac{1}{4}$in oversize all the way round. It can be worked with a bandsaw or with scissors. Remove the sharp corner of the foam with scissors or it will show as a line across the top covering. Glue the foam to the plywood to prevent it shifting.

4 Cut the cover oversize. Work the top upside down. Pull out the centre of each side in turn firmly and tack or staple with a trigger gun. Check that the profile of the seat is correct.

5 Tack from the centre of each side towards the corner. Replace any offending staples where the cover is not tensioned satisfactorily.

6 Pull the corner hard and tack across.

7 Cut off the surplus covering by making three cuts.

8 & 9 Tuck the surplus under and pull top down and staple. This may require some time to obtain the best results.

GARDEN GATE

When the brace is in the position shown in the illustration the hinges must be fitted to the left-hand stile. Bevelling the top surfaces of all members helps to deflect the rain and prevent early rotting of the timber. The pailings can be fitted in shallow bare-faced mortises in the centre rail and then secured to the brace and bottom rail with screws.

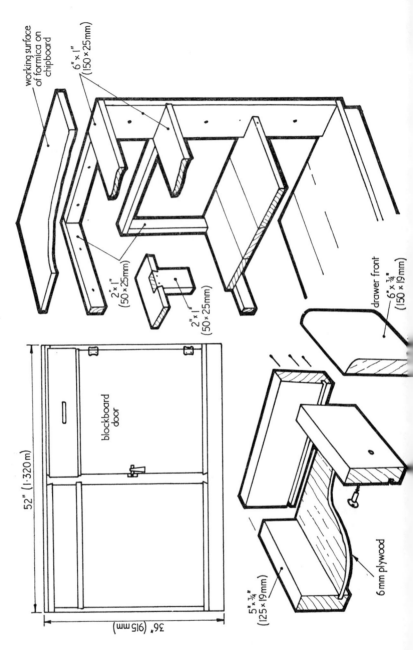

working surface of formica on chipboard

6" × 1"
(150 × 25mm)

2" × 1"
(50 × 25mm)

2" × 1"
(50 × 25mm)

drawer front
6" × ¾"
(150 × 19mm)

blockboard door

52" (1·320 m)

36" (915 mm)

5" × ¾"
(125 × 19mm)

6 mm plywood

Fig 125 Built in furniture. A guide to the construction of a cupboard

BUILT-IN FURNITURE

One example of built-in furniture has pinewood shelving coated with clear polyurethane varnish which is supported by battens plugged to the wall. The shelves are spaced to suit the items they have to contain.

Units built into the kitchen are also very popular. Figure 125 suggests one method of tackling this work. This will provide shelf and cupboard space, a simply made drawer, and a plastic-covered working surface.

DINING CHAIR

□ CUTTING LIST

Back legs	2	31½in (800mm)	x	4in (100mm)	x	⅞in (f) (22mm)
Front legs	2	18½in (470mm)	x	1¾in (f) (45mm)	x	⅞in (f) (22mm)
Side seat rails	2	16in (410mm)	x	2in (f) (50mm)	x	⅞in (f) (22mm)
Front, back seat rails	2	18in (460mm)	x	2in (f) (50mm)	x	⅞in (f) (22mm)
Bottom rails	3	18in (460mm)	x	1¼in (f) (32mm)	x	⅞in (f) (22mm)
Back rails	2	18in (460mm)	x	2in (f) (50mm)	x	2in (f) (50mm)

Materials for the seat are also required.

Consider the side frames first and make a start by planing the taper on the inside of the front legs. The bottom of the foot should finish 1⅛in (29mm) by ⅞in (22mm). Mark out the shaping on the back legs but shape only the inside surface of the back leg at this stage. If the whole of the shaping was done it would prove difficult to hold the back leg when cutting the joints.

Set out the wood for the side frames. Use a marking knife, sliding bevel and try square to mark the shoulder lines on the rails. Mark the mortise limit lines with pencil on the legs

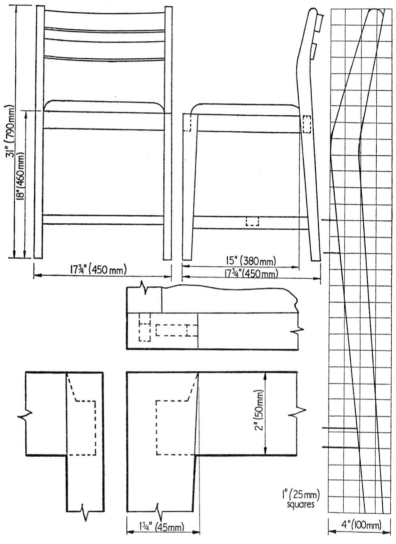

Fig 126 Dining chair

Gauge the four mortise and tenon joints on each frame. One joint will have a secret (sloping) haunch as illustrated, but the other three joints are straightforward stub mortise and tenon joints. Cut these joints then complete the shaping on the back legs. Remove most of the waste from the legs with a hand saw then place both legs together and clean them up with a spokeshave. This will ensure greater uniformity. If it is planned to make a set of these chairs a cardboard template for the back legs will prove helpful.

Clean up the inside surfaces, polish, and glue up the side frames before proceeding further.

Five rails are used to join the side frames together. These rails can be tenoned into the side frames. Alternatively, cut the rails accurately to length and dowel them in position. Take care to offset the joints on the ends of the back rails. The latter are next shaped to a smooth curve finishing each rail to $\frac{5}{8}$in (16mm) thick.

The seat is made from $\frac{1}{2}$in (12mm) plywood and is padded with foam. The covering material is wrapped over the foam and tacked underneath the plywood. Four wooden corner blocks are screwed inside the chair frame $\frac{1}{2}$in (12mm) below the top edge of the seat rails. These blocks support the seat and strengthen the chair.

MAKING AND FITTING A DRAWER

To make a drawer that works is one of the most difficult woodworking operations. The following is offered as a guide to the person who seeks this challenge.

A good quality drawer is held together by dovetail joints. A lap dovetail joint is used at the front of the drawer as this conceals the joint and gives a better appearance. Through dovetails are used at the back of the drawer. Tradition dictates that the bottom of the drawer is made from solid wood, though plywood does offer a good alternative. The grain of the bottom of the drawer must run from side to side of the drawer and never front to back. The bottom is fitted in a groove. This allows a solid timber bottom to expand out the back of the drawer, the drawer back being narrower than the sides and

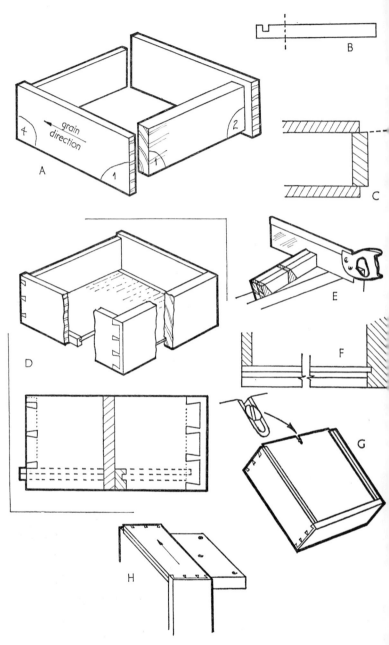

Fig 127 Making and fitting a drawer

allowing this to happen. Quite often the drawer sides are made from this material $\frac{5}{16}$in (18mm) thick. To increase the wear resistance of the drawer a slip of wood is glued to the side. This slip can carry the groove for the drawer bottom.

1   Select the timber for direction of grain. It is helpful when planing the sides of the drawer if the grain runs from the front of the drawer to the back. Quarter sawn oak is best for the side rails. Choose these out of stuff at least $\frac{5}{8}$in (16mm) too wide. Curly grain timber can be used for the drawer bottom. Mark the lower outside corners as shown.

2   Plane up the inside faces of the drawer using a trying plane.

3   Square the bottom edges of the side rails.

4   Plough a $\frac{1}{8}$in (3mm) groove in the drawer side and saw for the side slips. It is easier to groove a wide piece of wood and saw off the piece required than it is to plough a groove in a very small section of wood (fig 128b).

5   Plane a face edge on the drawer sides.

6   Gauge and plane the drawer sides to width so that they just fit inside the carcase.

7   Plane the bottom edge of the front piece square and to the shape of the carcase.

8   Plane one end of the front piece to fit the carcase and plane the other end likewise so that the front is a snug fit lengthwise.

9   Plane the front piece to width to fit the carcase. Make the top edge one shaving out of square so that the drawer front enters for only half its thickness (fig 127c).

10   Plough a groove on the inside of the front piece. This will receive the drawer bottom. Allow at least $\frac{1}{4}$in (6mm) underneath the bottom for drawer stops.

11   Plane the back rail to width (usually $\frac{1}{2}$in [13mm] narrower than the drawer sides) and to a tight fit lengthwise.

12   Gauge the front and back rails for length of pin. The side rails are at present thicker than they will finish so set the cutting gauge to the final thickness of the side rails.

13   Gauge for length of tail across the end grain of the front rail (usually $\frac{2}{3}$ thickness of the front rail).

P

14 Saw the sides to length (somewhat shorter than the depth of the carcase). Place these together in the vice and plane the ends square.

15 Gauge the length of tails around both pieces.

16 Mark out the tails. Allow for the groove in the front rail, and for the fact that the back rail is narrow (fig 127d).

17 Saw the tails together (fig 127e).

18 Separate the pieces and remove the waste from between the tails in the normal way.

19 Mark the pins from the tails using a scriber.

20 Cut the pins. This is straightforward with the through dovetail joint at the back of the drawer, but the lap dovetail on the drawer front is a little more difficult. Cramp the work flat on the edge of the bench and saw down the sides of the joint as far as possible. This will be an angle cut on the waste side of the lines. The rest of the waste has to be removed with a chisel. Work downwards across the grain then into the joint from the end. Make sure the chiselled surfaces are vertical then fit the joint.

21 Polish the inside surfaces of the drawer but avoid polish on the joints and where the slips are to be glued.

22 Glue up using a hammer and block of wood to close the joint. Use sash cramps just to squeeze out the excess glue. Check the diagonals to ensure the drawer is square, and check the drawer for wind (twist). Leave for the glue to dry.

23 Cut the drawer slips to length. Fit them, then glue and cramp them in place (fig 127f).

24 Plane the drawer bottom to remove any saw marks. It may be necessary to glue several pieces together to make one wide board. Check that the direction of grain will be across the drawer.

25 Rebate the ends of the drawer bottom to form a tongue that will fit the groove in the drawer slips. Slide the bottom in place and mark the front edge of the drawer. Plane this edge true then rebate so that the bottom fits into the groove on the front. Glue the drawer at the front corners and along the front edge of the drawer. Fit one or more slotted screws in the underside back (fig 127g).

26   Plane down the sides to the end grain of the front and back pieces. Use a trying plane and a planing block screwed to the bench top. Plane from the front of the drawer to the back.

27   Place the drawer in position and plane the front level with the carcase. A little *Ronuk* rubbed onto the drawer will make it work well.

CHILD'S DESK

☐   CUTTING LIST

Sides	2	$20\frac{1}{2}$in (520mm)	x	4in (100mm)	x	$\frac{5}{8}$in (f) (15mm)
Ends	2	$16\frac{1}{2}$in (420mm)	x	4in (100mm)	x	$\frac{5}{8}$in (f) (15mm)
Top	1	21in (f) (533mm)	x	17in (f) (430mm)	x	12mm plywood
Bottom	1	$20\frac{1}{4}$in(f) (540mm)	x	$16\frac{1}{4}$in(f) (412mm)	x	4mm plywood
Back	1	$21\frac{1}{2}$in (545mm)	x	$1\frac{1}{2}$in (f) (38mm)	x	$\frac{5}{8}$in (f) (15mm)
Legs	4	$21\frac{1}{2}$in (545mm)	x	2in (50mm)	x	1in (25mm)
Rails	2	9in (230mm)	x	2in (50mm)	x	1in (25mm)

Construction starts on this desk by making a framework with the corners joined by through dovetail joints. A plywood bottom that is attached to the framework with panel pins provides extra rigidity. The top should be sawn 4in (100mm) from the long edge and a piano hinge inserted along this cut. This will make an opening lid, the back portion being attached to the framework with screws.

The legs can be attached to the rails using either a secret (sloping) haunched mortise and tenon joint or a dowel joint. The shoulder line for the joint on the rail should be marked out to a slope of 1 in 14 using a sliding bevel. Attach the legs to the desk by screwing from the inside of the framework.

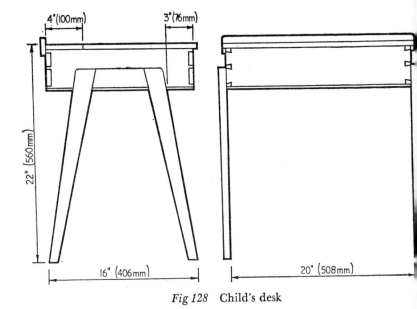

4"(100mm) 3"(76mm)

22" (560mm)

16" (406mm) 20" (508mm)

Fig 128   Child's desk

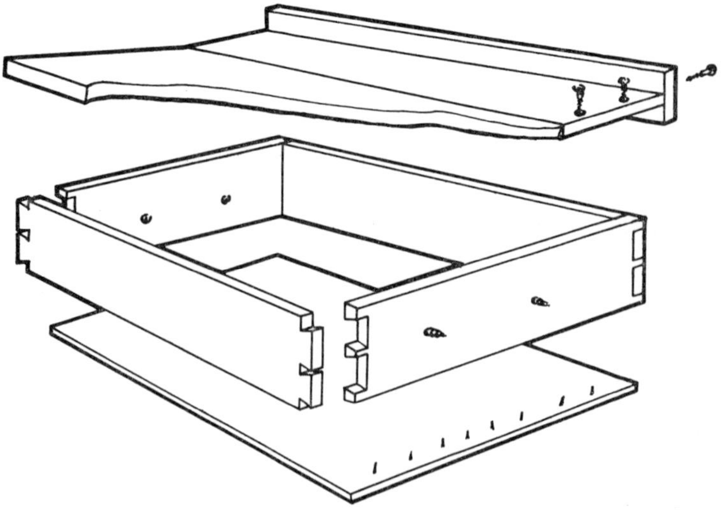

Fig 129   Child's desk. Exploded view

Appendix A

This list is given as a guide. It represents the tools that can form the nucleus of a kit.

Only the best tools should be bought. It is better to pay good money for tools now than discover later that your tools are inferior in quality. Always buy branded goods. Brands that can be recommended are Disston, Eclipse, Irwin USA, Marples, Millers Falls USA, Moore & Wright, Record, Ridgway, Stanley, Spear & Jackson, Woden.

The similarity in appearance between steel planes of different manufacture is very noticeable. The designer of the modern steel plane was Bailey, an American. He spent many years with Stanley Works USA. When the patent expired, planes of the Bailey design became manufactured by other firms. Some firms retain the original system of numbering the planes, eg 04, 05. Today the name Bailey can still be seen on the body casting of the planes produced by Stanley Works GB.

Crosscut handsaw	22in (560mm)	10ppi

(can be used for ripping, crosscutting and for cutting plywood)

Tenon saw	10in (250mm)	15ppi
Dovetail saw	8in (200mm)	18ppi

Coping saw and 10 blades

Firmer chisels	$\frac{5}{8}$in (16mm), 1in (25mm)
Bevelled edge chisels	$\frac{3}{16}$in (5mm), $\frac{1}{4}$in (6mm), $\frac{1}{2}$in (13mm)
Mortise chisels	$\frac{1}{4}$in (6mm), $\frac{5}{16}$in (8mm)
Steel jack plane	no 05$\frac{1}{2}$ - 15in (380mm) x 2$\frac{3}{8}$in (60mm)
Steel smoothing plane	no 04 - 9$\frac{3}{4}$in (250mm) x 2in (50mm)
Steel shoulder plane	no 041 - $\frac{5}{8}$in (16mm)

Spokeshave, flat, metal

Spokeshave, small round, wood

Marking knife (or small penknife)

Steel rule   12in (300mm)

'Pull-push' tape rule   6ft (2m)

Try square   6in (150mm)

Marking gauge

Mortise gauge, screw adjustment

Cutting gauge

Sliding bevel

Hand drill

Twist drills, high speed steel (HSS)
$\frac{1}{16}$in (2mm), $\frac{1}{8}$in (3mm)
$\frac{3}{16}$in (5mm), $\frac{1}{4}$in (6mm)

Round shank countersink bit

Brace and bits

Cabinet screwdriver   8in (200mm)

Mallet   5in (130mm)

Warrington hammer   14oz (400g)

Cork block

Medium oilstone   8in (200mm) x 2in (50mm) x 1in (25mm)

Appendix B

SOME SUPPLIERS

Timber, veneer, glue, fittings
   The Art Veneers Company Ltd, Industrial Estate, Mildenhall, Suffolk

'Tanalised' timber
   Dartington Timberwork Ltd, Court Street Sawmill, Moretonhampstead, Devon

Lubysil 717 and Lubysil G P I grease
   Silicone Lubrications Ltd, Thame House, Castle Street, High Wycombe, Bucks

Briwax
   Henry Flack Ltd, Croydon Road, Elmers End, Beckenham, Kent

Protective eye shields
   Safety Products Ltd, Redhill, Surrey

Reading List

☐   Books that are specially recommended are indicated by an asterisk.

*Abbatt, L. *The Stanley Books of Designs for Making your Own Furniture* (1969)

*Bradshaw, A. E. *Handmade Woodwork of the Twentieth Century* (1965)

Brazier, G. W. and Harris, N. A. *Woodwork* (1958)

Brown, W. H. *An Introduction to the Seasoning of Timber* (1964)

Clifford, N. C. E. *Timber Identification* (1957)

*Glenister, S. H. *Contemporary Design in Woodwork* Vol 1-3 (1955, 1961, 1968)

Hampton, C. W. and Clifford, E. *Planecraft* (Sheffield, 1960)

Hayward, C. H. *The ABC of Woodwork* (1960)

Hayward, C. H. *Cabinet Making for Beginners* (1960)

Hayward, C. H. *Tools for Woodwork* (1960)

Hayward, C. H. *Woodwork Joints* (1960)

*Hayward, C. H. *The Woodworker's Pocket Book* (1959)

*Laic, L. H. and Jones, D. A. *Designing in Wood* (1968)

Lewis, A. W. and Lewis, S. H. *Woodwork Drawing* (1966)

Mager, N. H. *How to Work with Tools and Wood* (New York, 1965)

*Moody, Ella. *Modern Furniture* (1966)

*Rowntree, Diana. *Interior Design* (1964)

Webster, Constance. *Timbers and Board Materials used in the Furniture Industry* (1966)

*Winter, E. *The Stanley Book of Designs for Home Storage* (1970)

☐   Periodicals of interest

Craft Education   *Do It Yourself*

Practical Woodworking   *Woodworker*

Acknowledgements

Mr D. B. Fisher, Public Relations Executive, Stanley Works (GB) Ltd, Sheffield

Archibald Kenrick & Sons Ltd, West Bromwich, Staffordshire

Borden Chemical Company (UK) Ltd, North Baddesley, Southampton

CIBA (ARL) Ltd, Duxford, Cambridge

English Abrasives Ltd, Marsh Lane, Tottenham, London

Evode Ltd, Stafford

Forestry Commission, 25 Savile Row, London

Formica Ltd, De la Rue House, London

G.K.N. Screws & Fasteners Ltd, Smethwick, Worcs

J. Glikstein & Son Ltd, Carpenters Road, London

C. & J. Hampton Ltd, Parkway Works, Sheffield

Irwin Auger Bit Company, Wilmington, Ohio, USA

Izal Ltd, Thorncliffe, Sheffield

Millers Falls, Greenfield, Massachusetts, USA

Moore & Wright (Sheffield) Ltd, Handsworth Road, Sheffield

James Neil & Co (Sheffield) Ltd, Napier Street, Sheffield

Silicone Lubrications Ltd, High Wycombe, Bucks

Smith & Davis Ltd, Beacon Works, Wednesbury, Staffordshire

Spear & Jackson Ltd, Aetna Works, Sheffield

Stanley Works (USA), New Britain, Conn, USA

General Index

Timber Index

.